FRONTERA

Margaritas, Guacamoles *and* Snacks

ALSO BY RICK BAYLESS

Fiesta at Rick's
(with Deann Groen Bayless)

Mexican Everyday
(with Deann Groen Bayless)

Rick and Lanie's Excellent Kitchen Adventures
(with Lanie Bayless and Deann Groen Bayless)

Mexico—One Plate at a Time
(with JeanMarie Brownson and Deann Groen Bayless)

Salsas That Cook
(with JeanMarie Brownson and Deann Groen Bayless)

Rick Bayless's Mexican Kitchen
(with Deann Groen Bayless and JeanMarie Brownson)

Authentic Mexican
(with Deann Groen Bayless)

Rick Bayless with Deann Groen Bayless

FRONTERA

Margaritas, Guacamoles *and* Snacks

Photographs by Paul Elledge

W. W. NORTON & COMPANY
NEW YORK | LONDON

For information about permission to reproduce selections from this book,
write to Permissions, W. W. Norton & Company, Inc.,
500 Fifth Avenue, New York, NY 10110

For information about special discounts for bulk purchases, please contact
W. W. Norton Special Sales at specialsales@wwnorton.com or 800-233-4830

Manufacturing by RR Donnelley, Crawfordsville, IN
Book design by Level, Calistoga, CA
Production manager: Anna Oler

ISBN 978-0-393-08892-2 (hardcover)

W. W. Norton & Company, Inc.
500 Fifth Avenue, New York, N.Y. 10110
www.wwnorton.com

W. W. Norton & Company Ltd.
Castle House, 75/76 Wells Street, London W1T 3QT

1 2 3 4 5 6 7 8 9 0

To the artisan tequila and mezcal producers
for the thrill concentrated in every sip,

To the craftsman avocado growers
for the luxury of texture and flavor,

And to Margarita, whoever she was.

{ contents }

Acknowledgments

For nearly three decades, my career as a cookbook author has been intertwined with—and benefited from—the vision, impeccable attention to detail and unwavering standards of Maria Guarnaschelli, editor extraordinaire. She is unparalleled as "reader-cook advocate," working through each recipe from scratch, pointing out the imprecise and cryptic, always striving to ensure delicious success for all who carry my recipes into the kitchen. Thank you, Maria.

And to you too, Doe Coover, who offer the constant wisdom, needed encouragement and welcome support necessary to keep me on track, draw the book to completion and get it into the hands of those who've been looking for just this title.

Jordan Johnston, our mixologist at Frontera, worked tirelessly with Deann and me developing a great many of the tequila and mezcal cocktails included here. We're indebted to his creativity, perseverance and ongoing passion for creating perfect cocktails.

Carlos Alferez, Frontera's general manager and partner, jump-started our tequila and mezcal program years ago. Shaw Lash, one of our development chefs at Frontera, took the ideas spun by so many of us chefs and created carefully tested recipes from them.

Jen Fite, our partner who brings together so many aspects of the Frontera world, skillfully shepherded this project to its beautiful conclusion. And Jeff Maimon, our personal assistant, juggled more schedules and tastings and ingredients and photos than anyone could have imagined. To all our staff who have so generously supported us as we bring Mexico's spirited inspirations alive in Chicago, we owe a huge debt of gratitude.

As my words were transformed into finished pages, magic happened. Paul Elledge's photographs brilliantly infused the book with mouthwatering beauty and the true flavor of Frontera culture; in fact, Paul and his wife (and partner), Leasha Overturf, have become so beloved here that we consider them special members of the Frontera family. And Level Inc. in Calistoga, CA, created a design to embrace all those words and images that's as perfectly good-spirited as I feel when having a margarita and some guacamole.

Brynne Rinderknecht stepped up to the plate to deliver some amazing props and styling suggestions, scouring Chicago for the perfect glass, plate, or pitcher. We thank her for the many miles she logged in her searches, and throw out a special nod to some of the companies that loaned us props for the shoot: Crosell & Co., Tabula Tua, Joseph the Butler, and P.O.S.H Chicago.

All books are a huge team effort. At Norton we are also grateful to a host of regulars who have time and time again helped us achieve our goals, from managing editor Nancy Palmquist and project editors Susan Sanfrey and Don Rifkin, to production and art department personnel including Anna Oler and Ingsu Liu, to Maria's unflappable and ever cheerful assistant Melanie Tortoroli, to our champion of sales and all-around morale booster Bill Rusin. Our thanks to all of them . . . and everyone else on the Norton team.

Lastly, I have three special "thank yous." The first is to Ron Cooper, who has for decades now championed artisan mezcal from Oaxaca, teaching us all of that libation's possibilities, if we just open our eyes to what's right in front of us.

For a quarter century or more, many folks have been doing that for tequila, since tequila began to shed its spring-break reputation and be recognized for its utterly enchanting character. But it's our current crop of mixologists—bartenders with deep knowledge, passion and creativity—that have brought new life to cocktails. We all owe them a hearty ¡Salud!

I've always been in love with guacamole—anything with avocado, really—but it wasn't until I started working with Alejandrina avocados from Uruapan, Michoacan, that I realized the full potential of a perfectly raised, coddled, carefully ripened one. When I visited their avocado groves, I recognized what an important role soil and climate play in creating incomparable flavor and texture. To the folks at Alejandrina and all the other craftsmen who labor with dedication and skill in the avocado fields: Thank you for bringing such pleasure to our lives.

Introduction

When my wife, Deann, and I opened Frontera Grill in 1987, after having spent a number of years living in Mexico, we had a single goal: to bring the then little-known regional flavors of Mexico to an audience we guessed wouldn't have tasted them, an audience we were convinced would fall in love with them as we had. Downtown Chicago became our location of choice for several reasons: Chicago has the second-largest concentration of Mexican immigrants in the United States, which, happily for us, meant an easy availability of ingredients. Plus, we had the support of Deann's family there and a burgeoning group of diners who were very enthusiastic about new restaurants offering something beyond the steak-and-potatoes fare Chicago was known for.

In many ways, except for a very few exceptions, the 1980s were the antithesis of today's locavore, farm-to-table restaurant culture. In fact, when we opened our restaurant's doors, all notable Chicago chefs prided themselves in sourcing their key ingredients from exotic locales.

While living in Mexico, I'd become steeped in a different way of thinking. There I'd learned that the most varied, most delicious regional cuisines flourished from a special synergy between the cooks and the local growers and producers, resulting, after many generations, in sound and very pleasurable traditions for nourishing the community.

Nevertheless, I knew that if I wanted my restaurant to be taken seriously in Chicago in 1987, I needed to create an "authentic" dining experience for my guests, and that most of them would understand that to include a menu of imported ingredients turned into faithful, "museum-quality" reproductions of dishes I'd tasted in Mexico. My heart sank. That kind of restaurant—one that serves "classic" dishes that most diners have never tasted before, made from ingredients far from their source—seemed artificial, cut off from its lifeline. Cuisine, to stay alive and vigorous, must be an ongoing dialog between cooks and diners, reflecting culture and place.

I quickly realized that striving for out-of-context authenticity was like chasing a shadow, a distant memory. Without all the freshest ingredients from the locale that had given life to a dish—without the locals to cook and eat the dishes, without the unique

scent of the place—there was no way to match my Mexican experience. Think about a simple plate of chilaquiles made from those crispy Oaxacan heirloom corn tortillas simmered in a sauce of local Zapotec pleated tomatoes. It's seasoned with smoky dried Oaxacan pasilla chiles and epazote; I've developed a Chicago source for the chiles, but the epazote grown in Oaxacan soil tastes considerably different from what I grow in my backyard. And the plate's garnish of thick cream and cheese from local grassfed herds has flavors I've tasted only there. Trying to create a pitch-perfect version of that everyday Oaxacan dish in Chicago would be pointless, impossible.

There is one thing I could strive for: deliciousness. I could create an utterly delicious plate of chilaquiles. I could make it from the best ingredients available to me, ingredients that are first and foremost chosen from my local Chicago seasonal bounty—crafted by dedicated artisans. And for ingredients we can't produce in Chicago, we'd search for ones that could withstand transportation and ones from small artisan producers that we could get to know personally. That wonderful plate of chilaquiles would pay unwavering respect to the Mexican culinary tradition I'd studied for years. But, as with any passionate cook, the dish would be expressed through my hands; it would express my vision (both traditional and contemporary) and communicate to my customers about my love and passion for Mexican flavor and culture.

This book is a perfect expression of the Frontera spirit. It's filled with delicious creations we make in Chicago, inspired by three muses: by the lively Mexican traditions of guacamole, tequila and spicy nuts, vegetables and fruits from street stalls; by our amazing local growers and producers; and by our passionate guests, who've been smitten with Mexican culture through its flavors and textures.

In the summer, when our local little pickling cucumbers are at their peak, we feature them in, among a dozen other dishes, the refreshing *agua fresca* of cucumber and lime. Everyone looks forward to the gingery cocktail we make from the *agua fresca*. And they look forward to using slices of those little cucumbers, fine-textured and velvety,

to scoop up a thick guacamole that sparkles with the spiciness of wild local watercress and nutty sesame. Those flavors and textures are the perfect marriage of Mexico and Chicago.

In the winter, we get the most flavorful little tangerines from Beck Groves, a biodynamic farm near San Diego. Their juice makes a perfect winter refreshment in the form of a tangerine margarita laced with a spiced triple sec. Tasting a chipful of toasted almond guacamole (dotted with bits of Beck Grove grapefruit) along with a sip of that tangerine margarita is a lesson in the satisfaction of seasonal eating and drinking in Chicago, Mexican style. Guacamole made with pinkish, out-of-season tomatoes and margaritas blended from bottled sweet-and-sour mix always leave me hungry, no matter how much I've had.

These days, great ingredients are available everywhere in the United States—in farmers' markets and supermarkets that pride themselves on bringing beautifully crafted and cultivated ingredients to local cooks. I hope that our Frontera inspirations will encourage you to search out all that's unique to where you cook, and from them to create your own lively and delectable versions of the Mexican classics.

one

Classic Margaritas

A Master Class
in Margaritas

When I'm yearning to make myself the perfect margarita, I find it useful to apply a little thought and science to the dynamic and pleasure-provoking art of mixology. After all, making a margarita is basically just mixing three ingredients: lime, tequila and orange liqueur. If you count additional sweetener, ice and a salted rim on the glass, you're still only at six ingredients—ingredients that are almost begging for some deliberation and balance. And if there's one lesson my decades-long kitchen-and-bar apprenticeship has taught me, it's this: the fewer ingredients you have in a dish or drink, the more intimate your knowledge of each must be and the more delicate their balance.

Odd as it may seem to some people, for me a margarita's most important ingredient is the **lime juice**. I first have to determine whether or not I'm going to be able to lay my hands on the tiny Key limes or if I'll be using the everyday grocery store hybrid limes, the ones typically just labeled "limes" (though distributors know them as Persian, Tahitian or Bearss limes). I also have to decide whether I want the more distinctive aroma and

the extra touch of tang and bitterness I'll get from the Keys or am looking for a more mellow lime that'll allow the tequila to shine.

Now, before you jump ship, deciding that even the lime decision is more than you're willing to consider, just know that I'm sympathetic. I've drunk margaritas made by self-professed margarita geeks who applied so much thought and science to their endeavor that they took all of the delicious fun out of it. I'm really not that kind of cocktail maker— I'm all about soul-satisfying deliciousness— though you may not believe me when reading the next sentence. When I make margaritas, I actually think about how ripe the limes are, the way I choose to juice them and the freshness of the juice I use. In brief, here are my concerns. *All* limes mature from green to yellow (most of us never see them fully ripened), and in ripening, they develop a less acidic and more flowery-aromatic flavor. Key limes are noticeably better, in my opinion, when they are at the "breaking" stage, between green and yellow. If I use an electric or manual cone-shaped juicer or a handheld reamer, I get beautiful, light-tasting juice. If I use a Mexican lime squeezer (my favorite), I crush the skin while squeezing out the juice, allowing some of the aromatic oils to mix in—translat-

ing into more complex, flavorful juice. Most grocery-store fresh-squeezed lime juice has a bitterness that seems to be the result of both squeezing method and how long ago it was juiced. My home-squeezed juice, even when refrigerated for up to two days, never develops that kind of bitterness. In fact, lime juice mellows a bit after being squeezed—a flavor you might like when creating a smooth margarita. That's why I don't hesitate to squeeze the limes up to two days ahead and store the juice, *tightly covered*, in the refrigerator.

When making margaritas for a special occasion, I'm typically striving for smoothness, for that "Whoa, silky!" comment, for that guttural sigh that lets me know my guests have fallen for my seduction. That means I'd choose the mellower hybrid limes rather than Key limes, maybe buying them a few days early so that they can ripen and sweeten up a touch on the counter. And I'd juice them a day ahead, using a reamer or Mexican lime juicer, and store the juice in the refrigerator.

The natural tang of any fresh lime juice in a margarita needs a little tempering with **a sweetener**—simple syrup, agave syrup or just plain sugar. **Simple syrup** provides a silky texture, especially when made rich (mix 2 cups sugar and 1 cup water in a saucepan and set over medium-high heat, stirring until the sugar dissolves and the mixture reaches a boil; let cool, stirring occasionally). You'll get the best flavor if the sugar you use is organic evaporated cane juice, and the syrup's color will be amber. **Agave syrup** provides that silky texture too. Though most are very light in flavor, the Wholesome Sweeteners organic light agave syrup has a pale amber color and rich flavor (it reminds me a little of light maple syrup) and is best in margaritas that feature aged tequilas. **Sugar** works fine, though I'd use superfine sugar just to ensure that it dissolves completely when added directly to a drink. Or you can follow the technique we've developed at our restaurant and combine the lime, sugar and water into a **homemade sweet-and-sour mix** (it's really just a strong *limonada*—fresh limeade). Our recipe, which yields 2¾ cups, calls for mixing together 1 cup fresh lime juice, ½ cup sugar and 1½ cups water, stirring until the sugar is completely dissolved; cover and refrigerate until you're ready to make cocktails.

Next I choose my **tequila**. Most of us are familiar with the age classifications for tequila: Blanco/silver is the youngest, typically bottled within 2 months of being distilled. Reposado is slightly aged, having spent 2 to 12 months in oak barrels of any size and any age (many have been used so often that tequila makers consider them neutral in flavor). Añejo has been aged for at least a year in small oak barrels; and extra-añejo has stayed in those barrels for at least 3 years. It's true: the more age, the smoother the texture. But in a margarita, are the subtleties, complexity, ultrasmoothness and value of an añejo or extra-añejo going to shine? Probably not, so I look for something in the reposado category—a tequila that's certainly smoother and less bright than a blanco—and one that's been aged in newer or smaller barrels for a little extra richness.

My fourth choice is the **orange liqueur**, of course, and I'm always surprised at how little importance most folks place on its selection. There are dozens of options, and almost every one of them will nudge a margarita's taste in a different direction. To make things easy to comprehend, I think of orange liqueurs as divided into triple secs (clear or artificially colored orange liqueurs) and orange-infused brandies like Grand Marnier, Gran Gala and Torres Orange. The triple sec category is the most varied: There are easy-to-find, inexpensive, mass-produced, simple-tasting, low-alcohol versions; I think of them as orange-flavored simple syrup with a little kick. And then there are the triple secs to be reckoned with, the ones like orange Curaçao that come in at 40% alcohol and focus on single varieties of aromatic-skin oranges or weave together a variety of those oranges (almost all include the superaromatic bitter oranges). For most folks, Cointreau still reigns over this category.

The orange-flavored brandies are all serious libations—there are no mass-produced versions I know of—and they offer a seamless mash-up of brandy, special oranges, sweetness and, occasionally, herbs and spices. When I'm making a margarita with one of them, I'm creating a drink that's different from the standard bright-and-refreshing version. I am creating a margarita around the brandy's richness and depth. Sometimes I find Grand Marnier's rich, caramely flavor a little domineering; Torres Orange is lighter and typically easier to blend to a perfect balance.

Proportions

A margarita is built basically like any "sour" drink—think whiskey sour, old-fashioned daiquiri, gin fizz, caipirinha. I agree with the venerable Dale DeGroff in *The Craft of the Cocktail* that a good, crowd-pleasing, starting-point **proportion** for all these drinks is 1½ to 2 ounces base liquor, ¾ ounce sour ingredient(s) and 1 ounce sweet ingredient(s). From there you can fine-tune, especially since not all sour ingredients will be of equal strength and sweetness can come in many forms and guises.

With those proportions in mind, consider the classic recipe for the margarita, the one many claim is the original: 1 ounce each blanco tequila, orange liqueur and fresh-squeezed Key lime juice. It'll be a tart drink for sure (an ounce of lime juice instead of ¾ ounce, and Key limes are the tangiest of all). And unless your orange liqueur has a muscley sweetness (like orange Curaçao or Cointreau), the lime will dominate. And if you don't use an orange liqueur that's close to 80 proof, you may think the drink tastes weak. Still, when only the most refreshing, bracing margarita will do, nothing beats a margarita that combines equal parts of a bright highlands blanco tequila like El Tesoro, Cointreau and fresh-squeezed lime. Shake it with ice for 15 seconds, and you'll have some people's favorite margarita of all time.

Which brings me to the **ice**. I'll apologize beforehand to those for whom a discussion of ice quality in cocktail making is deeper than they think anyone should delve. If that's you, just skip over the next paragraph and on to my words about the importance of shaking a margarita.

My bottom-line ice rules: (1) fresh ice tastes better than what's been hanging out in the freezer for a week or two; (2) smaller cubes melt faster than larger cubes, meaning more dilution when shaken with a cocktail; (3) ice cubes made from filtered or distilled water taste purer/cleaner/more satisfying than those made from tap water; and (4) clear ice cubes—made from boiled water— are prettier and look very professional. For everyday use, the ice I find in my refrigera-

tor ice maker is fine as long as it's fresh—it's filtered water made into cloudy medium-size cubes. But when I want to make the best margarita for a special occasion, I freeze larger cubes made from boiled filtered water (boiling releases air trapped in the water, air which would cloud the cubes). I like 1-inch cubes and I make them in a silicone mold so they pop out easily; you can find molds online and at places where specialized cookware is sold.

The rhythm of table-side margarita shaking sets the pace of Frontera Grill and Topolobampo day and night. Why shake margaritas over ice? Why not just take the easier road and serve them on the rocks? There are at least four reasons **why shaking a margarita is so important**. Most of the bases I make are strong, fully blossoming only with the dilution they get as the ice begins to melt into the mixture during shaking. And during shaking, the drink gets really cold, making a refreshing cocktail even more refreshing. Little flecks of ice chip off the cubes, pass through the strainer and add texture to the drink. And shaking aerates the margarita, creating a light, attractive froth on top. When I'm making my perfect margarita, I'm shaking it.

The question left is, **"Salt or no salt?"** Personally, for most margaritas, I don't consider the salted glass rim an indulgence, a gilding of the lily. I consider salt as important in most margarita making as in good salsa making or good grilling. Without salt, you can produce a tasty creation . . . but not a drop-dead delicious one. More than any other distilled spirit, tequila has a flavor that pops when you add a little salt. Plus, the combination of lime and salt seasons half of what folks eat in Mexico. So salted-rim margaritas make sense from both a flavor and a cultural perspective.

I like using coarser varieties like kosher salt (or Maldon, if you're feeling flush), stick-ing the crystals to the rim of the glass by first rubbing it with or dipping it in lime juice. I can make a lighter coating with these larger crystals, which is what I like. But I want there to be enough salt that a few grains dissolve into the drink, which will happen even when I salt only half the rim. A half-salted rim gives me the option of throttling just how much salt I weave into the margarita's flavor.

Enough said. Today, the recipe that follows is perfect for me. Who knows what tomorrow will bring?

Measuring

When professional bartenders talk drink recipes, they talk in ounces or fractions thereof—not tablespoons, not fractions of a cup, not milliliters. For cooks at home (at least in the United States), ounces aren't frequently part of the jargon. In fact, when you stray away from drink recipes, the use of ounces can be confusing: Is the recipe writer calling for ounces by volume or weight? Most of the time, those yield very different results.

Still, this is a book that reflects the spirit of Frontera's bar, which is run by professional bartenders. So every recipe is written first in single-cocktail, bartender style—with ounces. Following the official bartender recipe, there's a batch recipe—most make 8 drinks—that'll call for more friendly cup measurements and be useful for those of us who want to make a delicious cocktail for a group of friends. At work, we use the bartender recipes, making cocktails one at a time for groups of guests who typically want a variety of cocktails; at home, I make a batch recipe and serve everyone the same cocktail. Well, sometimes I offer a couple of choices, but still based on the batch recipes.

Now, if you want to venture into the bartender recipes, you might want to invest in a jigger, but realize that there are 1-ounce, 1¼-ounce and 1½-ounce jiggers. Instead, I'd buy one of the little Oxo ¼-cup measures that has clearly marked ¼-, ½-, 1-, 1½-, and 2-ounce marks. Oxo also makes a great shaker, the top of which functions as a clearly marked, jigger-like measure.

Today's Perfect Margarita
(aka Topolo Margarita)

Bartender's Recipe
MAKES 1 COCKTAIL

Coarse (kosher) salt

1 lime wedge

1½ ounces Sauza Tres Generaciones tequila (100% agave resposado) or Sauza Conmemo-rative (a lighter-style añejo, which was our best option when we created this margarita twenty-five years ago)

2½ ounces *Limonada* (page 21)

⅓ ounce Torres Orange liqueur

6 to 10 ice cubes (about ¾ cup)

Spread the salt on a small plate. Moisten the rim of a 6-ounce martini glass with the lime wedge and upend the glass onto the salt to crust the rim.

In a cocktail shaker, combine the tequila, *Limonada*, orange liqueur and ice. Cover and shake vigorously until frothy and cold; tiny ice crystals will appear in the drink after about 15 seconds of shaking. Strain into the salt-crusted glass and serve immediately.

Pitcher Recipe for a Party
MAKES 8 COCKTAILS

1½ cups Sauza Tres Generaciones tequila (100% agave resposado) or Sauza Conmemora-tive (a lighter-style añejo; see Bartender's Recipe)

2½ cups *Limonada* (1 cup fresh lime juice mixed with ½ cup sugar and 1½ cups water will yield 2¾ cups, a little more than you need)

⅓ cup Torres Orange liqueur

1 lime wedge

Coarse (kosher) salt

6 cups ice cubes

In a pitcher, combine the tequila, *Limonada* and orange liqueur. (Or stir together the lime juice, sugar and water until dissolved before adding the remaining ingredients). Cover and refrigerate until chilled, about 2 hours.

Use the lime and salt to crust the rims of eight 6-ounce martini glasses as described in the Bartender's Recipe. Fill a cocktail shaker half full with ice and pour in a generous 1 cup of the margarita mixture. Shake and strain into two of the prepared glasses. Repeat for the remaining margaritas.

The Best Margarita on a Budget

Making a good margarita is never going to be cheap (it takes 8 to 12 years for agaves to mature before their labor-intensive harvest, roasting, fermentation and distillation—all reflected in the price), but knowing how to use the least expensive ones to their full advantage is a lesson worth learning. I'm suggesting you choose either El Jimador Blanco or Sauza Blue Agave Blanco 100% agave tequila, because they are reasonably priced, are widely available and have a bright, distinctive agave flavor. Vanilla-infused triple sec gives the delicious illusion that you're using a tequila of greater age, softness and . . . expense.

Bartender's Recipe

MAKES 1 COCKTAIL

BARTENDER'S NOTES: To make 1 cup Vanilla Triple Sec, split ½ vanilla bean in half lengthwise. Pour 1 cup triple sec into a glass container, add the 2 pieces of vanilla bean, cover and let steep for 24 hours. Remove the vanilla bean pieces, and the triple sec is ready to use. It will keep for a long time, but it loses its vibrancy in about 3 to 4 months.

Coarse (kosher) salt

1 lime wedge

1½ ounces 100% blue agave blanco tequila, such as El Jimador Blanco or Sauza Blue Agave Blanco

1 ounce fresh lime juice

½ ounce Vanilla Triple Sec (see Bartender's Notes)

½ ounce agave syrup (light organic syrup gives the best flavor) or Rich Simple Syrup (page 21)

6 to 10 ice cubes (about ¾ cup)

Spread the salt on a small plate. Moisten the rim of a 6-ounce martini glass with the lime wedge and upend the glass onto the salt to crust the rim.

In a cocktail shaker, combine the tequila, lime juice, Vanilla Triple Sec, agave or simple syrup and ice. Cover and shake vigorously until frothy and cold; tiny ice crystals will appear in the drink after about 15 seconds of shaking. Strain into the salt-crusted glass and serve immediately.

Pitcher Recipe for a Party

MAKES 8 COCKTAILS

1½ cups 100% blue agave blanco tequila, such as El Jimador blanco or Sauza Blue Agave blanco

1 cup fresh lime juice

½ cup Vanilla Triple Sec (see Bartender's Notes)

½ cup agave syrup (light organic syrup gives the best flavor) or Rich Simple Syrup (page 21)

1 lime wedge

Coarse (kosher) salt

6 cups ice cubes

In a pitcher, combine the tequila, lime juice, Vanilla Triple Sec and agave or simple syrup. Cover and refrigerate until chilled, about 2 hours.

Use the lime and salt to crust the rims of eight 6-ounce martini glasses as described in the Bartender's Recipe. Fill a cocktail shaker half full with ice and pour in a scant 1 cup of the margarita mixture. Shake and strain into two of the prepared glasses. Repeat for the remaining margaritas.

How Tequila Is Made

The way tequila is made is very different from, say, brandy or vodka or schnapps. With most distillates there's surprisingly little talk about the origin of what's being distilled. With vodkas, you sometimes don't even know if it's made from potatoes or grain, much less what kind of grain it is.

Tequila has another story, and it always begins with the agave. Where and how the agaves reach their full maturity—which takes 8 to 12 years, unlike the *yearly* harvest of grains, potatoes and grapes—tells you a lot about the finished product. The rest you learn from how those agaves are roasted, crushed, fermented, distilled and aged (or not).

Blue agave (*agave tequilana Weber var. azul*), the only variety that by law can be used to make tequila, echoes the flavors of the soil and climate in which it's been cultivated. Tequilas that are distilled from agaves grown in the iron-rich clay soil of the cooler, rainier highlands typically have a more floral, herbal and complex aroma and flavor. Those distilled from agaves grown in the warmer, more volcanic soil of the lowlands show off rustic qualities like cinnamon oil, mineral and earth. Most agave farmers will tell you that the tastiest plants are grown without crowding or pruning, so they can soak up the greatest amount of sun. And when they're given the luxury of coming to full maturity—meaning the moment before the huge flower spike emerges from the agave's heart—they'll have developed the greatest amount of potential sugar and the greatest complexity of flavor. That takes years to accomplish and a very practiced eye to discern and is the reason some folks say that tequila is aged in the plant, not the bottle.

When an agave is ready for harvest (and every harvest I've seen has been done by hand), the 50- to 150-pound (or larger) plant is hand-cut from its root by trained *jimadores* using a circular-shaped hoe called a *coa*. This takes incredible strength, as does the lopping off of all the spiky leaves (*pencas*). The heart of the agave—the leafless part that's called the *piña* because of its resemblance to a pineapple—is all that's used to make tequila.

In bygone days, the tequila hearts—usually halved or quartered—were roasted for days in wood-fired pits in the ground (that's still how agave is roasted for the more rustic Oaxacan mezcal). But by the mid-1800s, when tequila was beginning to distinguish itself from the more rustic agave-derived spirits of Mexico, the roasting process had been made more "modern" by roasting those hearts for several days in steamy, above-ground stone ovens—cleaner, easier, less smoky. Today, much of the agave is roasted in steamy autoclaves for a day or so, but more *tequileros* agree that this approach doesn't produce as flavorful a tequila as the more traditional oven-baked approach.

Once the roasted hearts have cooled and their natural starches have been converted to tasty sweetness, their juice needs to be extracted and fermented into alcohol before distillation. In other words, the tequila makers need to turn what has become agave sugar into a kind of agave "beer."

- Step one: Mash the fibrous roasted hearts to make the sugary juices more accessible. I've seen it done with mechanical shredders, wooden bats and the traditional *tahona*, a massively heavy rock wheel (it looks like a millstone on its side) that's pulled by horses round and round over the agave in a low circular trough. Some *tequileros* add water during the crushing process to extract more juice.
- Step two: Collect the released juices into a large vessel (with or without some of the fibers). I've seen everything from huge wooden barrels to stainless, fiberglass and cement. Some *tequileros* collect roasting juices from the oven to add to the fermentation tank; others add sugars (but only if they're making the less expensive, less distinctive *mixto* tequila). They need to add yeast too, if there isn't enough free-floating wild yeast in the atmosphere to start the fermentation.
- Step three: Allow the mixture to ferment until it has a strongly yeasty-beery aroma and almost no residual taste of sweetness—with natural yeast, this can take 3 days to a week depending on the ambient temperature and the yeast's liveliness; with commercial yeast, a full fermentation can be achieved in a day or two.

It's this agave "beer" that is the prize, the stuff that'll be distilled. Whether or not it's been fermented with the fibrous remnants of the agave heart will affect the final flavor of the tequila; how strenuously those fibers are pressed is a flavor-affecting factor too.

When the fermented wort, as it's typically called, is ready and strained, it's transferred to the still. Now, I think of a still as similar to a pressure cooker—a closed vessel in which liquidy stuff is brought to a boil. But unlike a pressure cooker, which traps the expanding, steamy liquid in the closed vessel, creating pressure, the still provides a single small escape at the top for steamy alcohol. This vapor contains more than just alcohol: it harbors the pure flavor essence of what's simmering below. That's what escapes into a tube that coils through a water bath, cooling the vapor to the point that it condenses into a potent clear liquid—nascent tequila—redolent of the roasted agave heart that gave it life. It runs out of the tube into a collection vessel. Tasting the warm, undiluted tequila directly from the still is unforgettable: it vaporizes on your tongue, exploding a magical flavor and sensation through your whole body.

Distilling the newly made tequila a second time—double distillation must be part of all distillates labeled tequila—refines and focuses the flavors even more. Some *tequileros* distill a third time for a lighter flavor (most *tequileros* think a third pass strips out too much agave flavor). Some add a portion of the fibrous heart (it's called *bagaso* at this point) to the still during distillation to extract even more agave flavor. And most are very finicky about just how much of the head and tail (the very different-tasting—not necessarily great-tasting—first and last liquid to come off a distillation run) they include in the finished tequila.

And, of course, distillers are picky about their stills. Artisanal stills are typically pot stills—those called alembic—made of copper. These artisanal stills vary considerably in size, but no matter what size, they produce a more complex-tasting libation than the continuous still (aka column) that is occasionally used for less-expensive distillates.

Once the elixir has exited the still for a second time, it is usually between 45 and 55 percent alcohol—stronger than what we typically buy. Some *tequileros* dilute it to the common 40 percent and bottle it right away, to sell as the ever-popular blanco (aka silver or *plata*) tequila. What's going to be aged into a reposado (2 to 12 months) or añejo (12–36 months) or extra-añejo (3 years or longer) usually gets aged at still-strength in wood; the maturation of reposados is allowed to happen in large casks (though some choose smaller barrels), while the añejos must rest in smaller barrels—none can exceed 600 liters.

This may all sound rather technical—maybe more than you ever thought you'd know about tequila making. Truthfully, though, I've only sketched out the basics of the complex science and art that goes into filling those bottles labeled 100% agave tequila.

My Idea of the
Best Splurge Margarita

Everyone has his or her own belief about amounts for the dream margarita, and, having polled dozens of margarita aficionados, I can tell you those beliefs vary widely. But when Jordan Johnston, Frontera's mixologist, made this resonant, silky-smooth version for me, I knew within seconds that it was *my* dream. Jordan knows how wild I am about the soft, symphonic flavor of Riazul añejo tequila—caramel, nuts, dried fruits, vanilla, agave—and its incredible suppleness from being aged in French Cognac barrels. Having sipped its perfectly beautiful depth and complexity, I would never have thought of mixing anything with it. But I was shortsighted. If you add just the right amount of Grand Marnier, fresh lime and sweetness, that superpremium Riazul blossoms even more beautifully. Honestly—and that's from someone who had to be convinced.

Bartender's Recipe

MAKES 1 COCKTAIL

BARTENDER'S NOTES: *This recipe has been carefully developed to focus and support the flavor of Riazul añejo tequila—meaning that Grand Marnier is necessary (no other orange liqueur worked well). Chances are, if you're splurging on all these fine ingredients, it's a special occasion; you may want to literally gild this lily with gold leaf flakes or dust (easily available online). And about salt: using it balances the drink's richness brilliantly, but that may not be exactly what you're looking for from this beauty.*

Coarse (kosher) salt (optional)

1 lime wedge (optional)

1½ ounces 100% blue agave Riazul añejo tequila

2 ounces *Limonada* (page 21)

½ ounce Grand Marnier

6 to 10 ice cubes (about ¾ cup)

Edible gold leaf flakes or dust (optional)

If you choose to have a salted rim, spread the salt on a small plate, moisten the rim of a 6-ounce martini glass with the lime wedge and upend the glass onto the salt to crust the rim.

In a cocktail shaker, combine the tequila, *Limonada*, Grand Marnier and ice. Cover and shake vigorously until frothy and cold; tiny ice crystals will appear in the drink after about 15 seconds of shaking. Strain into the prepared glass, sprinkle a little gold leaf or dust on top, if desired, and serve immediately.

Pitcher Recipe for a Party

MAKES 8 COCKTAILS

1½ cups 100% blue agave Riazul añejo tequila

2 cups *Limonada* (1 cup fresh lime juice mixed with ½ cup sugar and 1½ cups water will yield 2⅔ cups. Dilute the extra *Limonada* with a little sparkling water for a refreshing limeade while you are preparing for your party.)

½ cup Grand Marnier

1 lime wedge (optional)

Coarse (kosher) salt (optional)

6 cups ice cubes

Edible gold leaf flakes or dust (optional)

In a pitcher, combine the tequila, *Limonada* and Grand Marnier. Cover and refrigerate until chilled, about 2 hours.

If you choose to, use the lime and salt to crust the rims of eight 6-ounce martini glasses as described in the Bartender's Recipe. Fill a cocktail shaker half full with ice and pour in 1 cup of the margarita mixture. Shake, strain into two of the prepared glasses and sprinkle a little gold leaf or dust on top, if desired. Repeat for the remaining margaritas.

Limonada

(AKA FRONTERA'S SWEET-AND-SOUR MIX)

MAKES 2¾ CUPS

- 1 cup fresh lime juice
- ½ cup sugar

In a pitcher, stir the lime juice with the sugar and 1½ cups water until the sugar has dissolved. Cover and refrigerate until chilled. Fresh is best, but I think *Limonada* still tastes good after a couple of days in the refrigerator.

Rich Simple Syrup

MAKES ABOUT 2 CUPS

Choosing organic evaporated cane juice as the sugar for this recipe will give you the richest flavor. If you're used to making a single-strength simple syrup (1 part sugar to 1 part water), keep in mind that this recipe makes a double-strength version (2 parts sugar to 1 part water). This means less is necessary to sweeten a drink. This rich simple syrup is the only type that's called for in this book.

- 2 cups sugar

Measure 1 cup of water into a small saucepan, gently stir in the sugar, then set the pan over medium heat. Continue stirring gently (so you don't splash a lot of undissolved sugar crystals on the side of the pan) until the syrup reaches a boil and all the sugar has dissolved. Cool. Pour into a glass container, cover and store in the refrigerator. It will last for several months.

{ two }

Seasonal Fruit and Herb Margaritas

A s seasonal as our dining room menu is, you'd have expected us to have seasonal cocktails earlier than we did. Honestly, it was only a decade ago, after receiving a few cases of stunningly delicious biodynamic tangerines from Beck Grove, that we got the ball rolling. For me, tangerines are the most seductive of winter's fruit—the sticky sweetness of the sweet-and-sour citrus, the suppleness of the beautifully aromatic skin, the ruddy orange color. Tangerines bring sunniness to our less-than-sunny Chicago winters. To play both sides of northern freeze and Citrus Belt balm, our margarita infuses hearthside winter spices with fresh tangerine and lime.

Beck Grove sends us Meyer lemons too, and we showcase those in a winter margarita that captures their unique aroma. The glass can barely contain all the sunshine that pours from the shaker—Meyer lemon is infused into the tequila and simple syrup and squeezed into fresh juice.

I like all kinds of spice in the winter too, which is why I've slotted the Sparkling Ginger Margarita there. Truthfully, it is welcome during any season—warming in cool weather, refreshing when it's hot outside. There's a wry elegance to this cocktail, with its festive splash of sparkling wine followed by an unexpected fresh-ginger bite. Add the fresh kaffir lime leaf and it's elegantly exotic.

When our local farms have gone into hibernation, Frontera and Topolo feature a lot of tropical fruit, much of which is coming into the height of its season. While good pineapples are available to us most of the year, I'm most drawn to them in winter. I associate them with dreams of warm Mexican beaches dotted with street vendors selling slabs of that sweet fruit along with crunchy jícama and cucumber, all sprinkled with salt, crushed chile and lime. For anyone who's drawn to those elementally satisfying flavors, my (slightly savory) Pine-apple Margarita with Jícama, Cucumber and Crushed Chile is the cocktail to choose.

The arrival of the first spring strawberries from our Michigan farmers comes with all the energy, excitement and flourish of a trumpet fanfare. They are so remarkable, and the season is as fleeting as the spring blooms of crocus and lily of the valley. You can stretch the season with good strawberries from the grocery store, since the California season is longer than ours (look for ones grown in Baja too; they can be amazing). Always judge strawberries by aroma, not color.

But strawberries in a margarita? For most of us, the mere idea conjures up images of slushy sweetness hovering on the wrong side of natural. And for that very reason, it's taken me years to even consider any drink that pairs the words "strawberry" and "margarita." Then I tasted our mixologist Jordan Johnston's version, which blends in the delectable complexity of Aperol. I'm still not quite sure what to call it, other than amazingly good.

When spring strawberries are still weeks away, rhubarb is on every Chicago chef's menu: It's the first local "fruity" ingredient we have to cook with, and we work it into everything from salsas and pickles to braises and pies. Though it may not sound intuitively delicious to some of you, yes, we've even woven its tartness, with that unique hint of fruitiness, into cocktails . . . some more successfully than others. Once we discovered how to round out rhubarb's flavor with the depth of black currant and a brandy-based orange liqueur, we knew we'd found our drink. Not too rich, really satisfying, stunning to look at. Honest.

At the height of summer, our local peach season lasts a lot longer than the one for strawberries. And their sun-warmed ripeness is every bit as tasty. Laced with *hoja santa* (the large, anisey leaf from southern Mexico that I've figured out how to grow in profusion in my backyard), those peaches star in my favorite summer margarita. *Hoja santa* is hard to find, though, so I'm also giving you my second-favorite summer margarita: basil and peach, which leads to that same sort of enticingly savory twist that *hoja santa* does.

I live and cook near one of the great fruit-growing regions of our country: southwest Michigan. For over two decades, we've worked with Klug Family Farms, celebrating the flow from spring through summer to fall with hundreds of flats and cartons and crates of several dozen different fruits. Raspberries

signal that summer is in full swing (they also come back for a fall appearance). Macerated in blanco tequila, they give up their flavor and pinkish-red blush within a few days, creating a tequila that simply dances on your tongue. I like to throw in some lemongrass too, just to heighten the aromas, then use the infused tequila to make a pretty classic margarita, with just a touch of super-concentrated raspberry flavor from framboise. As you might imagine, the raspberry-lemongrass tequila is perfect for sipping as well as mixing.

In addition to their spice and green pepper freshness, jalapeños offer an appealing juicy crunch that's perfect for muddling. Add a little cilantro and salt, and you're halfway to the brightest, freshest salsa—and perfect flavors to marry with the herbal minerality of a Jalisco Highlands blanco tequila. The

Cilantro-Jalapeño Margarita is one of my favorite summer libations with *carne asada* tacos or chile-grilled fish.

Our fall farmers' markets—with their many aromatic apple varieties and scintillating heaps of chiles in every shade of sunset—make an apple-habanero margarita seem almost too obvious. Roasting apples and habaneros brings out a caramely sweetness to match the habanero's natural fruitiness. And there's nothing like that chile's bright heat with tequila, especially when it's tamed by the fruity sweetness and a splash of apple brandy.

During the fall in west-central Mexico, street vendors nestle bowls of multicolored peeled prickly pears into ice to entice passersby with their cool refreshment and beauty. If you've never tasted this cactus fruit, it offers a juicy uniqueness that always reminds me a little of watermelon or kiwi. The flavor pairs beautifully with blanco tequila, which is why I've included a prickly pear margarita recipe here. Look for prickly pears at Mexican markets or well-stocked groceries; California's season starts earlier and goes later than Mexico's. There are directions for making a ruby-colored infused tequila in that recipe too, flavored and colored with dried *jamaica* flavors. The stuff is stunning and delicious.

Tangerine Spice Margarita

(Winter)

Bartender's Recipe

MAKES 1 COCKTAIL

BARTENDER'S NOTES: *The allspice dram, an old classic from Jamaica, reinforces the spices in the triple sec; if you can't find it (or don't like the strong allspice note it adds), the drink will still be very good. To make Allspice Salt for crusting the glasses, mix ¼ cup each coarse (kosher) salt and sugar with 1 tablespoon coarsely ground allspice.*

Allspice dram (we use St. Elizabeth)

Allspice Salt (see Bartender's Notes) or
salt-and-sugar (equal proportions)

1 lime wedge

1½ ounces 100% blue agave reposado tequila
(see page 96)

1 ounce fresh tangerine juice

¼ ounce fresh lime juice

¾ ounce Spiced Triple Sec (page 31)

¼ ounce agave syrup (light organic syrup gives
the best flavor) or Rich Simple Syrup (page
21)

6 to 10 ice cubes (about ¾ cup)

Give a 6-ounce martini glass a rinse with the allspice dram (dribble a few drops into the glass and swirl it around to coat the interior). Spread the Allspice Salt on a small plate. Moisten the rim of the glass with the lime wedge and upend the glass onto the salt to crust the rim.

In a cocktail shaker, combine the tequila, tangerine juice, lime juice, Spiced Triple Sec, agave or simple syrup and ice. Cover and shake vigorously until frothy and cold; tiny ice crystals will appear in the drink after about 15 seconds of shaking. Strain into the prepared glass and serve immediately.

Pitcher Recipe for a Party

MAKES 8 COCKTAILS

1½ cups 100% blue agave reposado tequila (see page 96)

1 cup fresh tangerine juice

¼ cup fresh lime juice

¾ cup Spiced Triple Sec (page 31)

¼ cup agave syrup (light organic syrup gives the best flavor) or Rich Simple Syrup (page 21)

Allspice dram (we use St. Elizabeth)

1 lime wedge

Allspice Salt (see Bartender's Notes) or salt-and-sugar (equal proportions)

6 cups ice cubes

In a pitcher, combine the tequila, tangerine juice, lime juice, Spiced Triple Sec and agave or simple syrup. Stir well to combine, then cover and refrigerate until chilled, about 2 hours.

Give eight 6-ounce martini glasses a rinse with the allspice dram (dribble a few drops into each glass and swirl it around to coat the interior). Use the lime and Allspice Salt to crust the rims of the glasses as described in the Bartender's Recipe. Fill a cocktail shaker half full with ice and pour in 1 cup of the margarita mixture. Shake and strain into two of the prepared glasses. Repeat for the remaining margaritas.

Spiced Triple Sec

MAKES 1 CUP

This makes enough Spiced Triple Sec for about 10 drinks. Any extra could be used in your favorite (regular lime) margarita, especially if you add a splash of sweet vermouth. I find it easiest to crack the spices using a mortar and pestle or putting them together in a freezer bag and crushing them with a rolling pin, mallet or the side of a large knife.

- 1 cup triple sec
- ¼ teaspoon cracked black pepper
- 1 teaspoon cracked allspice berries
- 2 whole cloves, cracked
- A ½-inch piece of cinnamon stick (preferably Mexican *canela*) crushed into small pieces

In a bowl or bottle, combine the triple sec and spices, cover and let stand at room temperature for 24 hours for the spice flavors to infuse.

Strain the triple sec through a fine-mesh strainer, pour into a glass storage container and cover. It will keep for a long time, but it will lose some of its vibrancy after 3 to 4 months.

Meyer Lemon Margarita *(Winter)*

Bartender's Recipe

MAKES 1 COCKTAIL

BARTENDER'S NOTES: *While this cocktail is also tasty made with everyday lemons, when the strikingly aromatic Meyer lemons become available in early winter, it's worth celebrating their deliciousness with a Meyer lemon margarita. Until the last decade of the twentieth century, Meyer lemons were mostly ignored and thought to lack viability as a commercial crop—until food luminaries like Alice Waters and Martha Stewart began championing them. They are thought to be a cross between a lemon and an orange.*

You'll find that it pays off enormously to use the Meyer lemon in three ways in this drink: infused into tequila, made into a simple syrup and squeezed into fresh juice.

If the drink seems a bit tart for your taste, simply add a little more of the syrup before shaking. Or add a touch of sweetness by crusting the rims of the glasses by rubbing them with a lime wedge, then upending the glasses onto a plate of granulated or powdered sugar.

To make a lemon twist, warm a lemon under hot water for about 10 minutes. Cut off both ends and make a slit through the rind down the length of the lemon. Peel back the rind and remove the fruit. (You can cut the fruit in half and then juice it—easiest with a handheld Mexican citrus juicer.) Tightly roll up the lemon peel, then cut the roll into ¼-inch-wide slices. Let the tight curls open up loosely so they can be draped over the edge of each glass. One lemon will give you about 4 to 5 twists.

1½ ounces Meyer Lemon Tequila (page 37)

1 ounce fresh Meyer lemon juice

¾ ounce triple sec

½ ounce Meyer Lemon Simple Syrup (page 37)

6 to 10 ice cubes (about ¾ cup)

A lemon twist for garnish (see Bartender's
Notes)

In a cocktail shaker, combine the Meyer Lemon Tequila, lemon juice, triple sec, Meyer Lemon Simple Syrup and ice. Cover and shake vigorously until frothy and cold; tiny ice crystals will appear in the drink after about 15 seconds of shaking. Strain into a 6-ounce martini glass, garnish with the lemon twist and serve immediately.

Pitcher Recipe for a Party
MAKES 8 COCKTAILS

1½ cups Meyer Lemon Tequila (page 37)

1 cup fresh Meyer lemon juice (you will need
4 to 5 lemons)

¾ cup triple sec

½ cup Meyer Lemon Simple Syrup (page 37)

6 cups ice cubes

8 lemon twists for garnish (see Bartender's
Notes)

In a pitcher, combine the Meyer Lemon Tequila, lemon juice, triple sec and Meyer Lemon Simple Syrup. Cover and refrigerate until chilled, about 2 hours.

Fill a cocktail shaker half full with ice and pour in 1 cup of the margarita mixture. Shake, strain into two 6-ounce martini glasses and garnish each one with a twist. Repeat for the remaining margaritas.

Making a Lemon Twist

STEP 1 Cut off both ends of the lemon and make a slit through the rind down the length of the lemon.

STEP 2 Peel back the rind and remove the fruit.

STEP 3 Tightly roll the lemon peel.

STEP 4 Cut the roll into ⅛-inch slices.

Meyer Lemon Tequila

MAKES ONE 750-ML BOTTLE

- 8 Meyer lemons
- One 750-ml bottle 100% blue agave blanco tequila (see page 95)

Using a vegetable peeler, remove the zest (colored part only) from the lemons in big strips. Place in a glass jar, add the tequila and cover tightly. Let stand for 4 days for the flavors to blend, tipping the jar back and forth a couple of times each day.

Strain out the zest, and the tequila is ready to use. Stored in a glass container or its original bottle, it will keep its vibrant flavor for a month or two.

Meyer Lemon Simple Syrup

MAKES A SCANT 1 CUP

- 2 Meyer lemons   • 1 cup sugar

Use a vegetable peeler to remove the zest (colored part only) in large strips from the lemons. Measure the sugar and ½ cup water into a small saucepan, add the zest, set over medium heat and stir until the sugar is dissolved. When the mixture reaches a boil, reduce the heat to low and simmer for 2 minutes. Cool, then strain.

Pour the syrup into a storage container, cover and refrigerate until you are ready to use. It will keep for several weeks.

Sparkling Ginger Margarita

(Winter)

Bartender's Recipe

MAKES 1 COCKTAIL

BARTENDER'S NOTES: *We first made this cocktail without the kaffir lime, and it tasted so sophisticated and refreshing . . . like what I imagine people drinking in the Hamptons. Once we added the fresh kaffir lime leaf—available in most Asian markets and some well-stocked groceries—I was transported to one of those beautifully modern hotels in Bangkok.*

While the Ginger Syrup isn't exactly essential in this cocktail, it's very simple to make (after all, you'll have fresh ginger on hand), and it shows off a different side of ginger's flavor.

It's not easy to muddle all the ginger when you're making a pitcher of these margaritas. Though a blender doesn't achieve the same result, it can help with the task: Blend the ginger to a coarse puree with the tequila, then add the lime leaves and muddle them by hand before finishing the drink. Blending will make the ginger a more prominent flavor—not necessarily bad, just different—but don't be tempted to blend the leaves too.

2 slices ginger the thickness of a quarter (no need to peel), coarsely chopped

1 fresh kaffir lime leaf, cut in half where the leaf is indented (optional)

1½ ounces 100% blue agave blanco tequila (see page 95)

½ ounce fresh lime juice

½ ounce orange Curaçao or other triple sec

¼ ounce Ginger Agave Syrup (page 40)

6 to 10 ice cubes (about ¾ cup)

1 ounce sparkling wine, such as a cava from Spain

In the bottom of a cocktail shaker, muddle the ginger slices and 1 of the (optional) kaffir lime leaf halves with a cocktail muddler or a wooden spoon until the ginger is coarsely mashed. Add the tequila, lime juice, Curaçao, Ginger Agave Syrup and ice. Cover and shake vigorously until frothy and cold; tiny ice crystals will appear in the drink after about 15 seconds of shaking. Strain into a 6-ounce martini glass and top with the sparkling wine.

Bruise the other half of the lime leaf, if using, by slapping it between your palms to release the aroma. Float it on the top of the drink and serve immediately.

Pitcher Recipe for a Party
MAKES 8 COCKTAILS

16 slices ginger the thickness of a quarter (no need to peel), coarsely chopped

8 fresh kaffir lime leaves, cut in half where the leaf is indented (optional)

1½ cups 100% blue agave blanco tequila (see page 95)

½ cup fresh lime juice

½ cup orange Curaçao or other triple sec

¼ cup Ginger Agave Syrup (see recipe below)

6 cups ice cubes

1 cup sparkling wine, such as a cava from Spain

In the bottom of a pitcher, muddle the ginger and *half* of the (optional) kaffir lime leaves with a cocktail muddler or wooden spoon until the ginger is coarsely mashed (see Bartender's Notes). Add the tequila, lime juice, Curaçao and Ginger Agave Syrup. Stir, cover and refrigerate until chilled, about 2 hours.

Fill a cocktail shaker half full with ice and pour in ⅔ cup of the margarita mixture (be sure to include some of the muddled ginger and lime leaf). Shake and strain into two 6-ounce martini glasses, then top each with sparkling wine. Repeat for the remaining margaritas. If using the lime leaves, one by one bruise the remaining leaves by slapping them between your palms to release their aroma, and float a piece on top of each drink.

Ginger Agave Syrup
MAKES ABOUT ½ CUP

- ½ cup agave syrup (light organic syrup gives the best flavor) or Rich Simple Syrup (page 21)

- ¼ cup (about 1 ounce) finely chopped ginger (no need to peel it)

Measure the agave (or simple) syrup and 2 tablespoons water into a small saucepan. Set over medium heat and add the ginger. When the mixture reaches a simmer, time 2 minutes, then remove from the heat and cool to room temperature; strain.

The syrup will keep for a month or more, tightly covered, in the refrigerator.

Pineapple Margarita with Jícama, Cucumber and Crushed Chile

(Winter)

Bartender's Recipe

MAKES 1 COCKTAIL

BARTENDER'S NOTES: *Think of this as the cocktail version of my favorite Mexican street snack: pineapple, jícama and cucumber sprinkled with fresh lime, crushed chile and salt. Not only does it perfectly capture those sweet-savory-spicy-tangy flavors, but the blended pineapple gives the drink a smoothie-like frothiness that always brings a smile to my face.*

To make Guajillo Salt, mix 1 part pure crushed or powdered guajillo chile to 2 parts coarse (kosher) salt; add a little more chile if a little extra spiciness appeals to you. Árbol, cayenne or smoky chipotle chile can be used here, but they're much *spicier than guajillo. Ancho is another option, but it's less spicy than guajillo and less bright in flavor. You can make your own crushed or powdered guajillo chile by oven-toasting stemmed and seeded guajillos at 325 degrees until nearly crispy, about 15 minutes; cool, then pulverize as much as you like in an electric spice grinder or mortar.*

To make about 3 cups Pineapple Puree, peel and core ½ medium pineapple. Cut it into roughly 1-inch cubes (you'll have about 3½ cups) and place in a blender or food processor. Add ½ cup sugar and ½ cup water, cover and pulse until the pineapple is finely chopped, then process until smooth and foamy, usually a full minute. Strain into a sealable container and refrigerate until ready to use, up to 3 days. Any leftover pineapple puree can easily become an agua fresca *to serve over ice by stirring in sparkling or still water, fresh lime juice and a little more sugar if you think it necessary.*

Guajillo Salt (see Bartender's Notes) or coarse (kosher) salt

1 lime wedge

1½ ounces 100% blue agave reposado tequila (see page 96)

¾ ounce fresh lime juice

¾ ounce triple sec

1½ ounces Pineapple Puree (see Bartender's Notes)

6 to 10 ice cubes (about ¾ cup)

A couple pieces of cucumber (¼-inch-thick sticks, about 4 inches long) for garnish

A couple pieces of jícama (¼-inch-thick sticks, about 4 inches long) for garnish

Spread the Guajillo Salt on a small plate. Moisten the rim of a 6-ounce martini glass with the lime wedge and upend the glass onto the salt to crust the rim.

In a cocktail shaker, combine the tequila, lime juice, triple sec, Pineapple Puree and ice. Cover and shake vigorously until frothy and cold; tiny ice crystals will appear in the drink after about 15 seconds of shaking. Strain into the salt-crusted glass, garnish with the cucumber and jícama and serve immediately.

Pitcher Recipe for a Party
MAKES 8 COCKTAILS

1½ cups 100% blue agave reposado tequila (see page 96)

¾ cup fresh lime juice

¾ cup triple sec

1½ cups Pineapple Puree (see Bartender's Notes)

1 lime wedge

Guajillo Salt (see Bartender's Notes) or coarse (kosher) salt

6 cups ice cubes

About 16 pieces of cucumber (¼-inch-thick sticks, about 4 inches long) for garnish

About 16 pieces of jícama (¼-inch-thick sticks, about 4 inches long) for garnish

In a pitcher, combine the tequila, lime juice, triple sec and Pineapple Puree. Cover and refrigerate until chilled, about 2 hours.

Use the lime and salt to crust the rims of eight 6-ounce martini glasses as described in the Bartender's Recipe. Fill a cocktail shaker half full with ice and pour in a generous 1 cup of the margarita mixture. Shake and strain into two of the prepared glasses. Repeat for the remaining margaritas. Garnish each glass with a spear or two of cucumber and jícama.

Pineapple Margarita with Jícama, Cucumber and Crushed Chile (page 41) >>>

The Ultimate Strawberry Margarita *(Spring)*

Bartender's Recipe

MAKES 1 COCKTAIL

BARTENDER'S NOTES: *You have to make a choice in this unusually delicious strawberry margarita recipe: Do you want to put a laser focus on the strawberries (Fragoli wild strawberry liqueur is the pure essence of strawberry flavor) or enhance their beauty (Cointreau does that beautifully) or balance their wonderful sweetness with even more sophisticated complexity (Aperol is perfect for that)? A "fan-sliced" strawberry (cut into several slices from just under the leaf-capped crown toward the tip) makes a simple, tasty garnish wedged on the side of each glass.*

To make Strawberry Sugar, combine equal measures of freeze-dried strawberries (we use the Just Strawberries brand) and granulated sugar in an electric spice grinder or small food processor and pulverize.

To make about 2 cups Strawberry Puree, cut the leafy crowns off about 15 to 20 strawberries and cut them in half (you need about 3 cups halved strawberries). Scoop into a blender or food processor, add ½ cup sugar, cover and process until smooth. Pour into a storage container (strain the mixture if you think there may be unblended bits), cover and refrigerate until you are ready to use, up to 3 days.

Strawberry Sugar (see Bartender's Notes) or
   granulated sugar for crusting the glasses

1 lime wedge

1½ ounces 100% blue agave blanco tequila (see
   page 95)

¾ ounce fresh lime juice

1 ounce Aperol
   OR ½ ounce Aperol plus ½ ounce Cointreau
   OR ½ ounce Aperol plus ½ ounce Fragoli wild
   strawberry liqueur

1½ ounces Strawberry Puree (see Bartender's
   Notes)

6 to 10 ice cubes (about ¾ cup)

A strawberry fan for garnish (optional)

Spread the Strawberry Sugar on a small plate. Moisten the rim of a 6-ounce martini glass with the lime wedge and upend the glass onto the sugar to crust the rim.

In a cocktail shaker, combine the tequila, lime juice, Aperol (plus Cointreau or Fragoli, if using), Strawberry Puree and ice. Cover and shake vigorously until frothy and cold; tiny ice crystals will appear in the drink after about 15 seconds of shaking. Strain into the sugar-rimmed glass and serve immediately. Garnish with the strawberry, if you like.

Pitcher Recipe for a Party
MAKES 8 COCKTAILS

1½ cups 100% blue agave blanco tequila (see
   page 95)

¾ cup fresh lime juice

1 cup Aperol
   OR ½ cup Aperol plus ½ cup Cointreau
   OR ½ cup Aperol plus ½ cup Fragoli wild
   strawberry liqueur

1½ cups Strawberry Puree (see Bartender's
   Notes)

1 lime wedge

Strawberry Sugar (see Bartender's Notes) or
   granulated sugar

6 cups ice cubes

8 strawberry fans for garnish (optional)

In a pitcher, combine the tequila, lime juice, Aperol (plus Cointreau or Fragoli, if using) and Strawberry Puree. Cover and refrigerate until chilled, about 2 hours.

Use the lime and Strawberry Sugar to crust the rims of eight 6-ounce martini glasses as described in the Bartender's Recipe. Fill a cocktail shaker half full with ice and pour in a scant 1¼ cups of the margarita mixture. Shake and strain into two of the sugar-rimmed glasses. Repeat for the remaining margaritas. Garnish the margaritas with the strawberries, if you like.

Black Currant–Rhubarb Margarita
(Spring)
Bartender's Recipe
MAKES 1 COCKTAIL

BARTENDER'S NOTES: *Choose rhubarb with a lot of red in the stem to make a puree that's beautifully rosy. The puree's velvetiness gives the drink a very satisfying texture.*

Though in many cases I consider the salt on the rim of a margarita glass to be an essential ingredient for balancing the sweet tanginess of the drink or bringing out the flavor of the tequila, certain combinations of flavors just don't need it. That's the case with this luscious spring drink. However, you may want to crust the rim with the sweet-tang of jamaica sugar (see Bartender's Notes, page 65).

1½ ounces 100% blue agave blanco tequila (see page 95)

½ ounce fresh lime juice

½ ounce Torres Orange or other brandy-based orange liqueur

1 ounce Rhubarb Puree (page 48)

½ ounce crème de cassis (black currant liqueur—I typically use Jules Theuriet brand)

6 to 10 ice cubes (about ¾ cup)

In a cocktail shaker, combine the tequila, lime juice, orange liqueur, Rhubarb Puree, crème de cassis and ice. Cover and shake vigorously until frothy and cold; tiny ice crystals will appear in the drink after about 15 seconds of shaking. Strain into a 6-ounce martini glass and serve immediately.

Pitcher Recipe for a Party

MAKES 8 COCKTAILS

1½ cups 100% blue agave blanco tequila (see page 95)

½ cup fresh lime juice

½ cup Torres Orange or other brandy-based orange liqueur

1 cup Rhubarb Puree (see recipe below)

½ cup crème de cassis (black currant liqueur— I typically use Jules Theuriet brand)

About 6 cups ice cubes

In a pitcher, combine the tequila, lime juice, orange liqueur, Rhubarb Puree and crème de cassis. Cover and refrigerate until chilled, about 2 hours.

Fill a cocktail shaker half full with ice and pour in 1 cup of the margarita mixture. Shake and strain into two 6-ounce martini glasses. Repeat for the remaining margaritas.

Rhubarb Puree

MAKES ABOUT 1½ CUPS

• 3 medium stalks (9 to 10 ounces) fresh rhubarb   • 6 tablespoons sugar

Trim the ends from the rhubarb stalks and discard. Chop the trimmed rhubarb into ½-inch pieces (you will have about 2¼ cups). In a small saucepan, combine the rhubarb, sugar and ½ cup water. Bring to a boil, then simmer over medium heat until the rhubarb is so tender that it's beginning to fall apart, 10 to 15 minutes. Cool to tepid.

Scrape the rhubarb mixture into a blender or food processor and process until smooth. (Alternatively, you can use a handheld immersion blender to puree the rhubarb directly in the saucepan.) Scrape into a sealable container (strain if you think there may be unblended bits) and refrigerate until ready to use, up to 5 days.

Peach (or Mango)-Basil Margarita

(Summer)

Bartender's Recipe

MAKES 1 COCKTAIL

BARTENDER'S NOTES: *If you can lay your hands on the Mexican herb* hoja santa, *use 2 small pieces of the leaf instead of the basil to muddle into the drink. A couple of leaves can be used to make the salt, and a single leaf to make the syrup (see recipes on page 52).*

When I'm pressed for time, I skip the basil syrup (I use an equivalent amount of agave syrup instead) and I choose the simple coarse salt option. There are no options, however, when it comes to making the Peach Puree.

To make a generous cup of Peach (or Mango) Puree, you will need 1 pound (3 or 4) ripe peaches or ¾ pound (2 small) ripe mangos. Peel, remove the flesh from the pits, then roughly chop into 1-inch pieces (you'll need about 2 cups). Scoop the fruit into a food processor or blender, add about 2 tablespoons sugar, cover and process until completely smooth. Pour into a storage container (strain the mixture if you think there may be unblended bits), cover and refrigerate until you are ready to use, up to 3 days.

Basil Salt (page 52) or coarse (kosher) salt

1 lime wedge

2 fresh basil leaves

1½ ounces 100% blue agave blanco tequila (see page 95)

¾ ounce fresh lime juice

½ ounce triple sec

1 ounce Peach (or Mango) Puree (see Bartender's Notes)

¾ ounce Basil Syrup (page 52)

6 to 10 ice cubes (about ¾ cup)

Spread the Basil Salt on a small plate. Moisten the rim of a 6-ounce martini glass with the lime wedge and upend the glass onto the mixture to crust the rim.

In the bottom of a cocktail shaker, muddle the basil leaves with a cocktail muddler or a wooden spoon until roughly mashed. Add the tequila, lime juice, triple sec, Peach (or Mango) Puree, Basil Syrup and ice. Cover and shake vigorously until frothy and cold; tiny ice crystals will appear in the drink after about 15 seconds of shaking. Strain into the salt-crusted martini glass and serve immediately.

Pitcher Recipe for a Party

MAKES 8 COCKTAILS

16 fresh basil leaves

1½ cups 100% blue agave blanco tequila (see page 95)

¾ cup fresh lime juice

½ cup triple sec

1 cup Peach (or Mango) Puree (see Bartender's Notes)

¾ cup Basil Syrup (page 52)

1 lime wedge

Basil Salt (page 52) or coarse (kosher) salt

6 cups ice cubes

In the bottom of a pitcher, muddle the basil leaves with a cocktail muddler or wooden spoon until coarsely mashed. Add the tequila, lime juice, triple sec, Peach (or Mango) Puree and Basil Syrup. Cover and refrigerate until chilled, about 2 hours.

Use the lime and Basil Salt to crust the rims of eight 6-ounce martini glasses as described in the Bartender's Recipe. Fill a cocktail shaker half full with ice and pour in a generous 1 cup of the margarita mixture (be sure to include some of the muddled basil). Shake and strain into two of the salt-crusted glasses. Repeat for the remaining margaritas.

Basil Syrup

MAKES 1 CUP

- 1 cup sugar

- 1 basil sprig, leaves removed (about 7 leaves) and roughly chopped

Measure the sugar and ½ cup water into a small saucepan and set over medium heat. Add the basil and bring to a simmer. Cook for 2 minutes, then remove from the heat. Cool and strain.

The syrup will keep for several weeks in the refrigerator, tightly covered. (Drizzle any leftovers over halved peeled peaches and roast at 450 degrees until tender and browned: these are incredible served with ice cream.)

Basil Salt

MAKES ABOUT 6 TABLESPOONS

- One 12-ounce bunch fresh basil (about 10 sprigs)

- ¼ cup coarse (kosher) salt

Pull the basil leaves from the stems (you'll have 2 loosely packed cups). Line a rimmed baking sheet with a silicone mat or parchment paper and spread the leaves out on it in a single layer. Heat your oven to its lowest setting (160 degrees is ideal), then slide in the basil and heat it—really, it's dehydrating—until the leaves are dry, about 30 minutes. (If your oven has a convection fan, use it here.) Cool.

Using a small food processor, an electric spice grinder or a mortar and pestle, coarsely pulverize the dried basil (you'll get about 2 tablespoons), then stir into the coarse salt.

Raspberry-Lemongrass Margarita

(Summer)

Bartender's Recipe

MAKES 1 COCKTAIL

BARTENDER'S NOTES: *Raspberries are plain-and-simple delicious, especially—in my opinion—when their flavor is heightened with a little lime and sugar. Lemongrass adds neither acid nor sweet, so its presence may seem debatable—until you experience how the herb's lemon-limey aromatics can embellish and underscore what the lime juice adds.*

It's not easy to muddle all the lemongrass when you're making a pitcher, so you might want to employ the aid of a blender. Just keep in mind that blending will cause the lemongrass flavor to be stronger—not necessarily bad, just different.

Jamaica Sugar (see Bartender's Notes, page 65) or granulated sugar

1 lime wedge

A 1-inch piece of lemongrass, roughly chopped

1½ ounces Raspberry-Lemongrass Tequila (page 56)

1 ounce *Limonada* (page 21)

½ ounce triple sec

½ ounce framboise liqueur (I like Jules Theuriet brand)

6 to 10 ice cubes (about ¾ cup)

Spread the *Jamaica* Sugar on a small plate. Moisten the rim of a 6-ounce martini glass with the lime wedge and upend the glass onto the sugar to crust the rim.

In the bottom of a cocktail shaker, muddle the lemongrass with a cocktail muddler or a wooden spoon until roughly mashed. Add the tequila, *Limonada*, triple sec, framboise and ice. Cover and shake vigorously until frothy and cold; tiny ice crystals will appear in the drink after about 15 seconds of shaking. Strain into the prepared glass and serve immediately.

Pitcher Recipe for a Party

MAKES 8 COCKTAILS

A stalk of lemongrass, trimmed to about 8
  inches long, roughly chopped

1½ cups Raspberry-Lemongrass Tequila (page
  56)

1 cup *Limonada* (½ cup fresh lime juice mixed
  with ¼ cup sugar and ¾ cup water will yield
  1⅔ cups. Dilute leftover *Limonada* with a
  little sparkling water for a refreshing limeade
  while you are preparing for your party.)

½ cup triple sec

½ cup framboise liqueur (I like Jules Theuriet
  brand)

1 lime wedge

Jamaica Sugar (see Bartender's Notes, page
  65) or granulated sugar

6 cups ice cubes

In the bottom of a pitcher, muddle the lemongrass with a cocktail muddler or wooden spoon until coarsely mashed. (Alternatively, in a blender jar, combine the roughly chopped lemongrass with the tequila and pulse until coarsely pureed. Pour into a pitcher.) Add the infused tequila (if you haven't already), *Limonada*, triple sec and framboise. Stir, cover and refrigerate until chilled, about 2 hours.

Use the lime and *Jamaica* Sugar to crust the rims of eight 6-ounce martini glasses as described in the Bartender's Recipe. Fill a cocktail shaker half full with ice, and pour in a scant 1 cup of the margarita mixture (be sure to include some of the muddled lemongrass from the bottom of the pitcher). Shake and strain into two of the sugar-crusted glasses. Repeat for the remaining margaritas.

Raspberry-Lemongrass Tequila

MAKES ONE 750-ML BOTTLE

- One 750-ml bottle 100% blue agave blanco tequila (see page 95)
- 3 to 5 stalks lemongrass, chopped crosswise into ½-inch pieces
- 3 cups (12 ounces) raspberries

Pour the tequila into a medium (3-quart) saucepan, cover and warm slowly over low heat to about 160 degrees (hot to the touch), 5 to 7 minutes. Remove from the heat, add the lemongrass, re-cover and let steep as it cools to room temperature. Pour into a large glass container and scoop in the raspberries. Let the tequila stand with the raspberries and lemongrass for 4 days for the flavors to blend, tipping the jar back and forth a couple of times each day. Strain out the solids, and the infused tequila is ready. Stored, covered, in a glass container or the original bottle, it will keep its vibrant flavor for a month or two.

Cilantro-Jalapeño Margarita

(Summer)

Bartender's Recipe

MAKES 1 COCKTAIL

BARTENDER'S NOTES: *Jalapeños vary wildly in their spiciness (as does each person's penchant for that spiciness), so you'll want to taste the one you're using and determine what you think is the perfect amount. I really love the spicy, grassy-green freshness that jalapeño infuses into this libation, a flavor that's made all the more delicious by the bruised cilantro leaves. Salt is essential in this drink, in my opinion, because of the way it dances with the jalapeño and cilantro. If you have time, make the Cilantro Salt for a truly amazing experience.*

Cilantro Salt (page 60) or coarse (kosher) salt

1 lime wedge

1 to 3 thin slices jalapeño (from a jalapeño that has been stemmed, halved, seeded and sliced lengthwise)

2 fresh cilantro sprigs

1½ ounces 100% blue agave blanco tequila (see page 95)

1 ounce fresh lime juice

1 ounce Cointreau

½ ounce agave syrup (light organic syrup gives the best flavor) or Rich Simple Syrup (page 21)

6 to 10 ice cubes (about ¾ cup)

Spread the Cilantro Salt on a small plate. Moisten the rim of a 6-ounce martini glass with the lime wedge and upend the glass onto the salt to crust the rim.

In the bottom of a cocktail shaker, muddle the jalapeño and 1 of the cilantro sprigs with a cocktail muddler or a wooden spoon until roughly mashed. Add the tequila, lime juice, Cointreau, agave or simple syrup and ice. Cover and shake vigorously until frothy and cold; tiny ice crystals will appear in the drink after about 15 seconds of shaking.

Bruise the second sprig of cilantro by slapping it vigorously between your palms (this releases the aroma). Place in the salt-rimmed glass, strain the contents of the shaker into the glass and serve immediately.

Pitcher Recipe for a Party

MAKES 8 COCKTAILS

8 to 24 thin slices jalapeño (from a couple of jalapeños that have been stemmed, halved, seeded and sliced lengthwise)

16 fresh cilantro sprigs

1½ cups 100% blue agave blanco tequila (see page 95)

1 cup fresh lime juice

1 cup Cointreau

½ cup agave syrup (light organic syrup gives the best flavor) or Rich Simple Syrup (page 21)

Cilantro Salt (page 60) or coarse (kosher) salt

1 lime wedge

6 cups ice cubes

In the bottom of a pitcher, muddle the jalapeño and 8 of the cilantro sprigs with a cocktail muddler or wooden spoon until coarsely mashed. Add the tequila, lime juice, Cointreau and agave or simple syrup. Stir, cover and refrigerate until chilled, about 2 hours.

Use the lime and Cilantro Salt to crust the rims of eight 6-ounce martini glasses as described in the Bartender's Recipe. Bruise the remaining 8 cilantro sprigs one at a time by slapping them vigorously between your palms to release the aroma. Put an aromatic sprig in each of the salt-crusted glasses.

Fill a cocktail shaker half full with ice, and pour in 1 cup of the margarita mixture (be sure to include some of the muddled chile and cilantro from the bottom of the pitcher). Shake the margarita mixture and strain into two of the prepared glasses. Repeat for the remaining margaritas.

Cilantro Salt

MAKES ABOUT ¾ CUP

- 1 medium bunch fresh cilantro, leaves removed from stems (you'll need about 2 loosely packed cups of leaves)

- ½ cup coarse (kosher) salt

Line a rimmed baking sheet with a silicone mat or parchment paper and spread the cilantro leaves out on it in a single layer. Heat your oven to its lowest setting (160 degrees is ideal), then slide in the cilantro and heat it—really it's dehydrating—until the leaves are dry, about 30 minutes. (If your oven has a convection fan, use it here.) Cool.

Using a small food processor, an electric spice grinder or a mortar and pestle, coarsely pulverize the dried cilantro (you'll get about ¼ cup), then stir into the coarse salt.

Apple-Habanero Margarita *(Fall)*

Bartender's Recipe

MAKES 1 COCKTAIL

BARTENDER'S NOTES: *Habanero chiles, though thought of primarily in terms of their heat, are one of the most delicious chiles on earth—fruity, citrusy, wonderfully floral. And they pair perfectly with apples. So when you're at the fall farmers' market, buy your favorite apples and a few habaneros (both are in abundance at the same time) for this special cocktail—special for anyone who loves spicy. For me, half of an habanero is the right amount. I typically roast a whole habanero with the apples, then roughly chop it and add it to the pureed apples a little at a time until the flavor and heat are perfect; I encourage you to do the same. Combining apple brandy with the roasted apple puree gives this drink a rich, roasty flavor with hints of oakiness. A resonant reposado tequila fits in beautifully, offering an age-induced smoothness while preserving the tequila's agave flavor.*

To make Peppery Cinnamon Salt, mix 3 parts coarse (kosher) salt with 2 parts ground cinnamon (preferably freshly ground Mexican canela*) and 1 part freshly ground black pepper.*

Peppery Cinnamon Salt (see Bartender's Notes) or coarse (kosher) salt

1 lime wedge

1½ ounces 100% blue agave reposado tequila (see page 96)

¼ ounce fresh lime juice

½ ounce apple brandy (Calvados is the most famous one)

1½ ounces Apple-Habanero Puree (page 64)

6 to 10 ice cubes (about ¾ cup)

Spread the Peppery Cinnamon Salt on a small plate. Moisten the rim of a 6-ounce martini glass with the lime wedge and upend the glass onto the salt to crust the rim.

In a cocktail shaker, combine the tequila, lime juice, apple brandy, Apple-Habanero Puree and ice. Cover and shake vigorously until frothy and cold; tiny ice crystals will appear in the drink after about 15 seconds of shaking. Strain into the salt-crusted glass and serve immediately.

Pitcher Recipe for a Party

MAKES 8 COCKTAILS

1½ cups 100% blue agave reposado tequila (see page 96)

¼ cup fresh lime juice

½ cup apple brandy (Calvados is the most famous one)

1½ cups Apple-Habanero Puree (page 64)

1 lime wedge

Peppery Cinnamon Salt (see Bartender's Notes) or coarse (kosher) salt

6 cups ice cubes

In a pitcher, combine the tequila, lime juice, apple brandy and Apple-Habanero Puree. Cover and refrigerate until chilled, about 2 hours.

Use the lime and Peppery Cinnamon Salt to crust the rims of eight 6-ounce martini glasses as described in the Bartender's Recipe. Fill a cocktail shaker half full with ice and pour in a scant 1 cup of the margarita mixture. Shake and strain into two of the prepared glasses. Repeat for the remaining margaritas.

Apple-Habanero Puree

MAKES 1½ CUPS

- 2 large apples, peeled, quartered and cored—a tart apple like Granny Smith works best here (you need about 3½ cups of apple quarters)
- ¼ cup sugar
- ¼ to ½ fresh habanero chile, stemmed
- ¼ cup agave syrup (light organic syrup gives the best flavor) or Rich Simple Syrup (page 21)

Heat the oven to 400 degrees. Spread the apples on a rimmed baking sheet and sprinkle with the sugar, tossing them to coat evenly. Add the habanero to the baking sheet and slide into the oven. Roast for 20 minutes, then use a spatula to flip the apple pieces. Roast for another 20 minutes, or until the apples are lightly browned and completely soft. Remove them from the oven.

In a food processor or blender, process the roasted apples with the agave syrup or Rich Simple Syrup and ½ cup water until completely smooth. Chop the habanero (seeds and all), then add a portion to the apple puree—start with a quarter chile to make it a little spicy, half for the full experience. Process to blend thoroughly, then taste and add more habanero if you were too timid at first. Pulse to blend.

Pour into a storage container (strain the mixture if you think there may be unblended bits), cover and refrigerate until you are ready to use, up to 5 days.

Jamaica-Prickly Pear (Cactus Fruit) Margarita *(Fall)*

Bartender's Recipe

MAKES 1 COCKTAIL

BARTENDER'S NOTES: *At its best, this drink is made with several special preparations. At its simplest, it can be made with plain blanco tequila, prickly pear puree and granulated sugar for crusting the glass rim—sidestepping the* jamaica *altogether.*

Jamaica *is the dried calyx of a flower in the hibiscus family, and it's steeped into teas throughout the Caribbean, Mexico and, now, far beyond. If you drink herbal teas, you've likely had* jamaica, *though you may not have known it. It has a cranberry tanginess and a thrillingly crimson color.* Jamaica *is available at any Mexican market, many well-stocked groceries and, of course, online.*

To make Jamaica *Sugar, place ½ cup dried* jamaica *flowers in an electric spice grinder and coarsely pulverize. Mix with ½ cup sugar.*

There are two main types of prickly pear on the market: a deep crimson-colored one that's typically called "red," and a light greenish one that's called "white." The red one is really beautiful in this drink and has a deeper, richer flavor. There are a few frozen prickly pear purees available, though the good ones are expensive. My favorite is made by Perfect Purée (perfectpuree.com or amazon.com).

To make a generous cup of Prickly Pear Puree, peel 6 prickly pears: Cut a ½-inch slice off both ends of each prickly pear. One by one, peel the prickly pears: make a ½-inch-deep incision down one side (end to end), then peel away the thick rind. Roughly chop the fruit that's in the middle and scoop it into a food processor or blender and process to a smooth puree. Strain into a sealable container, cover and refrigerate until you are ready to use it, up to 3 days.

Jamaica Sugar (see Bartender's Notes) or
granulated sugar

1 lime wedge

1½ ounces *Jamaica* Tequila (see recipe below)

1 ounce fresh lime juice

½ ounce orange Curaçao or other triple sec

1 ounce Prickly Pear Puree (see Bartender's
Notes)

½ ounce agave syrup (light organic syrup gives
the best flavor) or Rich Simple Syrup (page
21)

6 to 10 ice cubes (about ¾ cup)

Spread the *Jamaica* Sugar on a small plate. Moisten the rim of a 6-ounce martini glass with the lime wedge and upend the glass onto the sugar to crust the rim.

In a cocktail shaker, combine the tequila, lime juice, Curaçao, Prickly Pear Puree, agave or simple syrup and ice. Cover and shake vigorously until frothy and cold; tiny ice crystals will appear in the drink after about 15 seconds of shaking. Strain into the sugar-crusted martini glass and serve immediately.

Jamaica Tequila

MAKES ABOUT 1½ CUPS

- 2 cups 100% blue agave blanco tequila (see page 95)
- 1½ cups (2 ounces) dried *jamaica* flowers

Measure the tequila into a small saucepan, cover and slowly warm over low heat to about 160 degrees (hot to the touch). Remove from the heat, add the *jamaica* flowers, re-cover and let steep for 10 to 15 minutes. Line a strainer with cheesecloth, pour the tequila through it, gather the corners of the cheesecloth and squeeze or wring out the flowers, extracting as much tequila as possible.

When the infused tequila has cooled, it's ready to use. Stored in a glass container, it will keep its vibrant flavor for a couple of months.

  Jamaica-Prickly Pear (Cactus Fruit) Margarita (page 65) >>>

Pitcher Recipe for a Party
MAKES 8 COCKTAILS

1½ cups *Jamaica* Tequila (page 66)

1 cup fresh lime juice

½ cup orange Curaçao or other triple sec

1 cup Prickly Pear Puree (see Bartender's
Notes)

½ cup agave syrup (light organic syrup gives
the best flavor) or Rich Simple Syrup (page
21)

1 lime wedge

Jamaica Sugar (see Bartender's Notes) or
granulated sugar

6 cups ice cubes

In a pitcher, combine the tequila, lime juice, Curaçao, Prickly Pear Puree and agave or simple syrup. Cover and refrigerate until chilled, about 2 hours.

Use the lime and *Jamaica* Sugar to crust the rims of eight 6-ounce martini glasses as described in the Bartender's Recipe. Fill a cocktail shaker half full with ice and pour in a generous 1 cup of the margarita mixture. Shake and strain into two of the sugar-crusted glasses and repeat for the remaining margaritas.

{ three }

Mezcal Margaritas

B ecause of its rustic, smoky, big-muscle characteristics, I consider mezcal as a bit of a loner, not always in the mood to play with others. Just a simple sip of beautifully made, small-batch mezcal—supported by a pinch of heady *sal de guzano* (a spicy salt made with toasted maguey worms) and maybe a squeeze of orange or lime—is as close to mezcal perfection as I can imagine.

So why even try lacing it into cocktails? Why not take the straight-sipper's high road and just drink the stuff? Because you'd miss the unexpected magic that happens when the right ingredients in the right proportions end up in a glass, the result remarkably delicious and unlike anything else.

That's what happened when we created the Oaxacan Gold Margarita, starting with a grilled pineapple puree scented with rich vanilla extract. We were amazed at how the smokiness of the pineapple danced seamlessly with the rich and smoky mezcal. This not-too-strong cocktail is a wonderful way to introduce folks to mezcal.

If you've ever tasted tamarind straight—that dark, tangy, sticky substance inside barky-looking tamarind pods—you know how rich and complex it is. Pure tamarind is figgy, thrillingly sour and slightly smoky, which is why, like grilled pineapple, it welcomes mezcal so beautifully. A little Cointreau and lime are all you need to lift and round out the flavors in a delicious Tamarind-Mezcal Margarita.

Every time I used mezcal to replace tequila in a classic margarita, the mezcal's muscley smoke seemed to take over. Until I tried some citrus bitters. I was astonished at how the bitters' complexity tamed that smoke, bringing everything into beautiful balance. That's how we came up with our Mezcal Margarita #2. Small-batch citrus bitters are available online and in well-stocked liquor stores these days (we like Bittercube and Bittermans), but I've included a recipe for our homemade version. I bought the unusual dry ingredients online, mixed up the base and let it stand for a few weeks. It's simple, though you have to plan ahead.

Our El Mural, named for a drink some restaurant cohorts and I enjoyed at the wonderful El Mural restaurant in Puebla, is all fresh and thirst-quenching, the perfect drink for a summer afternoon in the backyard. Its balance only seems right when made with a not-very-smoky mezcal, like the ones made in Puebla. Though those aren't really distrib-

uted in the United States, a nonsmoky mezcal made by Fidencio in Oaxaca is distributed north of the border. Or just make the drink with a blanco tequila, sit back and enjoy.

I've included the Absinthe-Mezcal Margarita as a little treasure for aficionados. It's quite a basic margarita really, with a little muddled mint as a fresh underscore of absinthe's herbal qualities, mezcal instead of tequila to match absinthe's complexity and, of course, a splash of absinthe to make everything sing together.

Oaxacan Gold Margarita

Bartender's Recipe

MAKES 1 COCKTAIL

BARTENDER'S NOTES: *Though this drink celebrates pineapple's natural sweetness, the fresh lime keeps it from drifting toward cloying. And the fragrant vanilla underscores mezcal's smoke beautifully. (Vanilla and pineapple—especially grilled, broiled or caramelized pineapple—is a match made in heaven.) I find that a little spice is welcome here too, so I often crust the rim of the glass with Chipotle Salt (see Bartender's Notes, page 81).*

1 ounce Oaxacan mezcal (see page 96)

½ ounce fresh lime juice

2½ ounces Grilled Pineapple–Vanilla Puree (page 76)

6 to 10 ice cubes (about ¾ cup)

In a cocktail shaker, combine the mezcal, lime juice, Grilled Pineapple–Vanilla Puree and ice. Cover and shake vigorously until frothy and cold; tiny ice crystals will appear in the drink after about 15 seconds of shaking. Strain into a 6-ounce martini glass and serve immediately.

Pitcher Recipe for a Party

MAKES 8 COCKTAILS

1 cup Oaxcan mezcal (see page 96)

½ cup fresh lime juice

2½ cups Grilled Pineapple–Vanilla Puree (page 76)

6 cups ice cubes

In a pitcher, combine the mezcal, lime juice, and Grilled Pineapple–Vanilla Puree. Stir well to combine, then cover and refrigerate until chilled, about 2 hours.

Fill a cocktail shaker half full with ice and pour in 1 cup of the margarita mixture. Shake and strain into two 6-ounce martini glasses. Repeat for the remaining margaritas.

Grilled Pineapple–Vanilla Puree

MAKES 2 CUPS

- ½ large ripe pineapple (the half should weigh about 1 pound), peeled and cut crosswise into 1-inch-thick pieces (no need to core)
- ½ cup sugar
- ¼ teaspoon pure vanilla extract, preferably Mexican, the most flowery of all the vanillas

Prepare a hot fire in a charcoal or wood-fired grill and let burn until you have hot ash-covered coals (you can use a gas grill or grill pan, but you'll sacrifice some of that intoxicating smoky flavor). Grill the pineapple pieces until they have developed grill marks and softened considerably, about 2 minutes per side. Roughly chop.

In a blender, combine the still-hot grilled pineapple with the sugar, vanilla extract and 1 cup water. Pulse until roughly chopped, then blend on high until smooth and foamy, usually a full minute. Strain into a storage container and cool, then cover and refrigerate until you are ready to use, up to 3 days.

Tequila and Mezcal

Because of the shoebox-size bar we started with at Frontera, the focus of our offerings was exclusively on tequila—not surprising to anyone—with a sideways glance at tequila's smokier cousin, mezcal. Mezcal because part of my heart resides in Oaxaca, the state most famous for its mezcales, even though I'd venture to say that most of our early guests had never heard of it. Or, if they had, what they'd heard wasn't necessarily complimentary, usually tinged with heathen references to worms and allusions to Malcolm Lowry psychodelia and craziness. All that's changing now: 100% agave tequila has shed the spirit's spring-break past, emerging with the true colors of a world-class spirit. And mezcal is right on its heels.

Still, not all of us are clear on the differences between run-of-the-mill, inexpensive *mixto* tequila and those labeled 100% agave, between the different classifications of tequila (blanco, reposado, añejo and extra-añejo) or, for that matter, between tequila and mezcal. Here's my cheat sheet.

Difference between Tequila and Mezcal: In the distant past, any spirit distilled from any variety of roasted, fermented agave (there are hundreds of varieties) was called "mezcal." But by the mid-1800s, the folks who made an out-of-the-ordinary mezcal around the small town of Tequila, Jalisco, decided that theirs deserved special distinction, and "mezcal de Tequila" was separated from all others since it was made from a single, particularly delicious variety of agave (officially named *agave tequilana Weber var. azul*—aka blue agave). These people—the Cuervo family, the Sauza family and Félix López of Hacienda San José del Refugio, now Herradura—were right: Their spirit was exceptional, and people everywhere started asking for the bottles from Tequila. This led to other distillers jumping on the bandwagon, calling their spirits "mezcal de Tequila" (or "tequila" for short), even if their distilleries were not around the town of Tequila. By the mid-1970s, spirits called "tequila" had been given a Denomination of Origin with an accompanying Norma Oficial Mexicana (NOM)—a Mexican federal regulation—that dictates where tequila can be made (only five states in Mexico: Jalisco, Guanajuato, Michoacan, Nayarit and Tamaulipas), what agave can be used (blue agave), how it has to be distilled (twice) and how many aging classifications it can have (four—blanco, reposado, añejo, extra-añejo).

Things are less straightforward with mezcal. It has a Denomination of Origin and NOM, too, but they're broader and younger. Mezcal can be officially produced in seven states (Oaxaca, Durango, Guerrero, San Luis Potosi, Zacatecas, Guanajuato and Tamaulipas), from a host of different agave varieties and using different techniques. The state that is most famous for its mezcal (and the one with the greatest number of producers and variations) is Oaxaca. But there are delicious mezcales from Sonora (bacanora), Jalisco (raicilla) and Chihuahua (sotol).

Classification of Tequilas: First, there are two main divisions into which all tequilas are divided: *mixto* tequilas and 100% agave tequilas. *Mixtos* are less expensive, less distinctive tequilas that stretch the agave by adding up to 49% sugars during the fermentation process (*jovenes*, a related variety, are typically the young *mixtos* we call "gold" in the United States because a caramel color has been added to give softness and

an aged appearance—you may have tasted these in your younger years). In this book, I focus only on tequila that's made with 100% agave because I believe that it alone offers the true tequila experience.

Now, on to the aging classifications for tequilas. Keep in mind that the aging times are shorter than for other spirits because you're starting with a much more flavorful beverage right out of the still: a very complex flavor develops in agaves over the 8- to 12-year growth of the plant, in contrast to the one-season growth of corn, wheat rye or barley (bourbon and whiskey) or of grapes (brandy) or of grains or potatoes (vodka).

Blanco (aka Silver or *Plata*) Tequila: This is tequila straight from the still, aged less than 2 months. It is the brightest-flavored tequila, often a little fiery, always rich and complex with agave flavor, and generally representative of the flavor of the soil and climate in which the agave has been grown. Jalisco highlands tequilas most commonly have floral and herbal aromas and flavors; Jalisco lowlands tequilas commonly hint at rustic characteristics like wet-clay earthiness and cinnamon oil. To me, these clearly apparent characteristics of *terroir* and careful horticulture are thoroughly captivating, characteristics that are subdued with wood-aging. Still, there are good reasons for aging.

Reposado Tequila: In Spanish, the word *reposado* translates as "rested," but when you're talking tequila, the resting time is short. Mexico's NOM specifies 2 to 12 months in oak, though the size of the vessel can be very large. Just a few short months in contact with oak and air are enough to take the just-distilled (read: fiery) edge off and mellow it a little. The newer, smaller and more heavily toasted the barrel, the more apparent the toasty, sweet oak flavor. This will be either a plus or a minus, depending on how in love you are with the pure agave flavor.

Añejo Tequila: *Añejo* means "aged" in Spanish, and according to the NOM, an *añejo* tequila has to be aged over a year in oak barrels that don't exceed 600 liters. Since a 600-liter barrel is about three times the size of a normal wine barrel (a *barrique*), the flavor effect of the oak can be subtle, nothing like that experienced from bourbon that's been long-aged in new *barrique*-size barrels. The best tequila producers typically age their finest tequilas in those smaller barrels—

though rarely are they new—and with each successive batch the wood gives off less soft, caramely, sweet-vanilla flavor. I tend to be drawn to the slightly leaner añejos in which the richness of oak doesn't obscure the agave flavor. As you can imagine, there is a lot of variety in añejo flavor.

Extra-Añejo: This new classification, added in the summer of 2006, is simply an añejo that's been aged at least 3 years—though by law the producer doesn't have to specify how much over the 3 years it's been in the 600-liter or smaller barrel. Many of the extra-añejos are made in a style that allows them to compete with brandies or whiskeys.

Mezcal

Mezcal can be made from a number of different agaves, though *espadín* is probably the most common one and *tobalá*, the small, wild-harvested variety, is the most prized. Until recently, all mezcals were unaged *blancos*—or, if they were aged, it certainly wasn't in wood. That's changing as more and more people are falling in love with mezcal. They want to know the spirit's full potential. So don't be surprised if you see the same classifications for mezcal that you see for tequila. Though I've occasionally seen mezcals from other Mexican states show up in the United States, it's still pretty uncommon. Most mezcal in our markets is from Oaxaca and most is distinguished by its rustic smokiness (tradition dictates that the agave hearts are roasted in a wood-fired pit). Some Oaxacan producers are experimenting with other roasting methods as well as different approaches to crushing, fermenting and distilling. At this point, the regulations aren't as strict as they are for tequila.

Tamarind-Mezcal Margarita

Bartender's Recipe

MAKES 1 COCKTAIL

BARTENDER'S NOTES: *To make Chipotle Salt, mix equal parts pure powdered chipotle chile and coarse (kosher) salt. For a less spicy version, start with half the amount of powdered chipotle and add more to taste.*

Chipotle Salt (see Bartender's Notes) or coarse
  (kosher) salt
1 lime wedge
2 ounces Tamarind Puree (page 84)
1 ounce Oaxacan mezcal (see page 96)
½ ounce Cointreau
¼ ounce agave syrup (light organic syrup gives
  the best flavor) or Rich Simple Syrup (page
  21)
6 to 10 ice cubes (about ¾ cup)

Spread the Chipotle Salt on a small plate. Moisten the rim of a 6-ounce martini glass with the lime wedge and upend the glass onto the salt to crust the rim.

In a cocktail shaker, combine the Tamarind Puree, mezcal, Cointreau, agave or simple syrup and ice. Cover and shake vigorously until frothy and cold; tiny ice crystals will appear in the drink after about 15 seconds of shaking. Strain into the salt-crusted glass and serve immediately.

Pitcher Recipe for a Party

MAKES 8 COCKTAILS

2 cups Tamarind Puree (page 84)

1 cup Oaxacan mezcal (see page 96)

½ cup Cointreau

¼ cup agave syrup (light organic syrup gives the best flavor) or Rich Simple Syrup (page 21)

1 lime wedge

Chipotle Salt (see Bartender's Notes) or coarse (kosher) salt

6 cups ice cubes

In a pitcher, combine the Tamarind Puree, mezcal, Cointreau and agave or simple syrup. Stir well to combine, then cover and refrigerate until chilled, about 2 hours.

Use the lime and Chipotle Salt to crust the rims of eight 6-ounce martini glasses as described in the Bartender's Recipe. Fill a cocktail shaker half full with ice and pour in a scant 1 cup of the margarita mixture. Shake and strain into two of the prepared glasses. Repeat for the remaining margaritas.

<<< Tamarind-Mezcal Margarita (page 81)

Tamarind Puree

MAKES 4 CUPS

Frozen tamarind pulp (available in Latin grocery stores) and pastes/concentrates (available in Latin and Southeast Asian groceries and online) vary wildly, so it's hard to write a recipe using them that I feel completely confident about. (I've listed brands that I've had good luck with.) Though it takes a little additional time, a puree made from barky tamarind pods nearly always comes out consistently.

• 1 pound (about 16 large) tamarind pods—flexible ones with shells that flake off easily
OR one 14-ounce bag frozen tamarind pulp (I buy Goya brand at my local Mexican grocery)
OR 7 ounces paste/concentrate (I have had good luck with Thailand Wet Tamarind brand)

For pods: To clean the tamarind pods, one at a time, hold a pod in one hand, loosen the stem with the other and then firmly pull out the stem and all the runners that trail down between the shell and pulp; peel off the shell. In a large non-aluminum saucepan, bring 4 cups water to a boil. Add the tamarind, remove from the heat and let stand until completely soft—1 to 2 hours, depending on the freshness of the pods. Using your hand or the back of a large spoon, thoroughly dislodge the softened brown tamarind pulp from the fibrous material and seeds. Strain into a large pitcher, discarding the solids. You should have 4 cups of tamarind puree; if you don't, add water to reach that quantity.

For frozen pulp: Simply blend the defrosted pulp with 2 generous cups of water to bring the quantity up to 4 cups. Pour into a large pitcher.

For paste/concentrate: In a blender, combine the tamarind paste/concentrate (if it's in a brick form, roughly cut it up) with a scant 4 cups of boiling water. Blend on high until creamy and mostly smooth (don't worry if you see seeds—they will be strained out). Pour the puree through a strainer into a pitcher, pressing on the solids with a wooden spoon or ladle; discard the solids. You should have about 4 cups.

No matter which version you've made, cover the pitcher of tamarind puree and refrigerate until you are ready to use, up to 3 days.

Mezcal Margarita #2

Bartender's Recipe

MAKES 1 COCKTAIL

BARTENDER'S NOTES: *As you read through this recipe, you'll notice that it mirrors pretty classic margarita proportions . . . with the addition of orange bitters. Bitters work their magic here, as they do in many drinks, by adding depth, complexity and balance to otherwise pretty simple ingredients. And when you're mixing a drink with mezcal, that depth, complexity and balance are the hardest parts to achieve.*

1½ ounces Oaxacan mezcal (see page 96)

2 ounces *Limonada* (page 21)

½ ounce triple sec

6 to 8 drops orange bitters (store-bought or homemade, page 88)

6 to 10 ice cubes (about ¾ cup)

About a heaping ¼ teaspoon orange zest (colored part only; I use a Microplane grater/ zester or a 5-hole zester to zest the orange directly into the drink)

In a cocktail shaker, combine the mezcal, *Limonada*, triple sec, orange bitters and ice. Cover and shake vigorously until frothy and cold; tiny ice crystals will appear in the drink after about 15 seconds of shaking. Strain into a 6-ounce martini glass. Add the orange zest and serve immediately.

Pitcher Recipe for a Party

MAKES 8 COCKTAILS

1½ cups Oaxacan mezcal (page 96)

2 cups *Limonada* (1 cup fresh lime juice mixed with ½ cup sugar and 1½ cups water will yield 2⅔ cups. Dilute the leftover *Limonada* with a little sparkling water for a refreshing limeade while you are preparing for your party.)

½ cup triple sec

50 to 60 drops (1½ to 2 teaspoons) orange bitters (store-bought or homemade, page 88)

6 cups ice

About 2 heaping teaspoons finely chopped orange zest (colored peel only)—I typically use a Microplane grater/zester or a 5-hole zester to remove it

In a pitcher, combine the mezcal, *Limonada*, triple sec and bitters. Stir well to combine, then cover and refrigerate until chilled, about 2 hours.

Fill a cocktail shaker half full with ice and pour in 1 cup of the margarita mixture. Shake and strain into two 6-ounce martini glasses. Add ¼ teaspoon orange zest to each glass and serve immediately. Repeat for the remaining margaritas.

Lime (or Orange) Bitters

MAKES ABOUT 2½ CUPS

I'll admit that most of the ingredients for making bitters won't be in your kitchen cabinets. But they're easily available online. You'll need a rectified spirit, which is a high-proof (at least 150-proof) alcohol, in which to infuse your bitters ingredients: Everclear and Spirytus are the most common brands in my area. These potent, nearly flavorless liquids are often called neutral grain spirits, and their high alcohol content both speeds along and then preserves flavor extraction. Once the alcohol has coaxed the essence from herbs, spices and roots, heat pulls out what's left—this time in water. Combining the high-octane infusion with the no-octane one produces a rounder, more interesting flavor . . . and, of course, lowers the alcohol content.

    I've called for one piece of fruit to be zested with a microplane or 5-hole zester, creating very fine zest. I specified the rest of the zest be removed in big strips and then roughly chopped. If all the zest is very fine, the bitters will be very cloudy. But a little fine zest increases the intensity of the lime or orange flavor.

- 8 large limes
  OR 6 medium oranges
- 1 stalk lemongrass, cut crosswise into ¼-inch pieces
- 1 tablespoon green cardamom (aka true cardamom) pods
- 1 teaspoon coriander seeds
- 3 bay leaves (dried or fresh), roughly broken
- 2 eucalyptus leaves (dried or fresh), roughly broken
- 1 teaspoon dried angelica root pieces
- 1 teaspoon dried dandelion root pieces
- ½ teaspoon dried gentian root pieces
- 2 cups rectified spirit (common options are Spirytus Rektyfikowany and Everclear)
- 2 tablespoons Rich Simple Syrup (page 21)

Zest one of the limes (or oranges) using a Microplane grater/zester or a 5-hole zester. Use a vegetable peeler to remove the zest (colored part only) from the remaining limes (or oranges), being careful to remove as little of the white pith as possible, and roughly chop it. Scoop into a 1-quart glass storage container with a lid.

Add the lemongrass, spices, herbs and roots to the container. Pour in the rectified spirit, cover and gently shake to mix everything together. Place in a cool, dry place out of the sun for 2 weeks, tipping it back and forth every day to mix the ingredients.

After 2 weeks, strain the mixture and pour the flavored spirit into another sealable glass container; set aside. Scrape the solids into a small saucepan, add 1 cup water and bring to a simmer. Allow to cool.

Pour the water, with the solids, into the original glass container, cover and shake several times. Place it in a cool place out of the sun for 1 week, tipping it back and forth every day to mix the ingredients.

Strain the water and mix the flavored water with the reserved flavored spirit. (We typically strain everything one last time through a cheesecloth-lined strainer to remove as much sediment as possible.) Stir in the simple syrup. Pour into a bottle with an eye-dropper lid or with a top for shaking out droplets (bitters are typically called for by the drop). The bitters will maintain their intense flavor for 6 months or more.

El Mural
Bartender's Recipe
MAKES 1 COCKTAIL

BARTENDER'S NOTES: *In the United States, I've only seen Oaxacan* sal de gusano *(chile salt with pulverized toasted maguey worms) in well-stocked Oaxacan groceries. Truthfully, the best plan is to go to Oaxaca, buy it in the 20 de Noviembre market just off the main square and bring it back in your suitcase. At least one can dream . . . and then wake up and realize that the simple Chipotle Salt on page 81 is a fine substitute.*

Though Oaxacan mezcal is Mexico's most famous, mezcal is made in many states, from a wide variety of agaves and in different styles, some much less smoky than others. This cocktail works best with the least-smoky mezcal, one they might call sin humo *(literally, "without smoke") in Mexico. For this style, the agave hearts are usually roasted in an oven instead of a wood-fired in-ground pit.*

NOTE: *I call for wedges of the citrus fruits here. To get the size pieces I used, cut each fruit into 8 wedges, then cut a piece from the wedge as specified.*

Sal de gusano (see Bartender's Notes), Chipotle Salt (see Bartender's Notes, page 81) or coarse (kosher) salt (optional)

1 lime wedge

¼ grapefruit wedge (cut from a small grapefruit)

½ orange wedge

1 teaspoon agave syrup (light organic syrup gives the best flavor) or Rich Simple Syrup (page 21)

1½ ounces nonsmoky mezcal, such as one from Puebla or San Luis Potosí or the Oaxacan Fidencio *"Sin Humo"* Espadín

1 ounce fresh grapefruit juice

1 ounce fresh orange juice

1 ounce fresh lime juice

6 to 10 ice cubes (about ¾ cup)

If desired, spread the salt on a small plate. Use the lime wedge to moisten the rim of a 10-ounce highball glass and upend the glass onto the salt to crust the rim.

In the bottom of the glass, using a cocktail muddler or wooden spoon, muddle the citrus wedges with the agave or simple syrup until juicy and aromatic. Add the mezcal, citrus juices and ice and stir well with a long spoon. Serve immediately.

Pitcher Recipe for a Party

MAKES 8 COCKTAILS

1½ cups nonsmoky mezcal, such as one from Puebla or San Luis Potosí or the Oaxacan Fidencio "*Sin Humo*" Espadín

1 cup fresh grapefruit juice

1 cup fresh orange juice

1 cup fresh lime juice

1 lime, cut into 8 wedges

Sal de gusano (see Bartender's Notes), Chipotle Salt (see Bartender's Notes, page 81) or coarse (kosher) salt (optional)

¼ small grapefruit, cut into 2 wedges

½ orange, cut into 4 wedges

8 teaspoons agave syrup (light organic syrup gives the best flavor) or Rich Simple Syrup (page 21)

About 3 cups ice cubes

In a pitcher, mix together the mezcal and citrus juices. Refrigerate.

If desired, use 1 of the lime wedges and the salt to crust the rims of eight 10-ounce highball glasses as described in the Bartender's Recipe.

Cut each of the 2 grapefruit wedges into 4 pieces; cut each of the 4 orange wedges in half. Place a piece of grapefruit, orange and lime in each of the prepared glasses; you'll have to use the lime wedge you used to moisten the glasses. Add a teaspoon of agave or simple syrup to each glass and muddle with a cocktail muddler or the back of a spoon until juicy and aromatic. Top with ice. Pour a generous ½ cup of the mezcal mixture into each glass, stir and serve.

Absinthe-Mezcal Margarita

Bartender's Recipe

MAKES 1 COCKTAIL

BARTENDER'S NOTES: *I doubt you'll be trying this cocktail unless you're already a fan of absinthe's supercomplex, anisey flavor. Which means you've probably got a bottle of absinthe in the liquor cabinet, ready to splash into the drink. If you don't, be aware that "inexpensive absinthe" is an oxymoron; if you find one that fits that description, it's probably just a bottle of flavored vodka and not the real, complex deal. Some like this drink with a salted rim because that focuses the drink's flavor more on the mezcal than the absinthe.*

2 large fresh mint leaves, roughly torn

1½ ounces Oaxacan mezcal (see page 96)

¾ ounce fresh lime juice

½ ounce orange Curaçao or triple sec

¼ ounce absinthe (Sirene, Lucid and Küber are common brands)

¼ ounce agave syrup (light organic syrup gives the best flavor) or Rich Simple Syrup (page 21)

6 to 10 ice cubes (about ¾ cup)

In the bottom of a cocktail shaker, muddle the mint with a cocktail muddler or a wooden spoon until coarsely mashed. Add the mezcal, lime juice, Curaçao or triple sec, absinthe, agave or simple syrup and ice. Cover and shake vigorously until frothy and cold; tiny ice crystals will appear in the drink after about 15 seconds of shaking. Strain into a 6-ounce martini glass and serve immediately.

Pitcher Recipe for a Party

MAKES 8 COCKTAILS

16 large fresh mint leaves

1½ cups Oaxacan mezcal (see page 96)

¾ cup fresh lime juice

½ cup orange Curaçao or triple sec

¼ cup absinthe (Sirene, Lucid and Küber are
common brands)

¼ cup agave syrup (light organic syrup gives
the best flavor) or Rich Simple Syrup (page
21)

6 cups ice cubes

In the bottom of a pitcher, muddle the mint with a cocktail muddler or wooden spoon until coarsely mashed. Add the mezcal, lime juice, Curaçao or triple sec, absinthe and agave or simple syrup. Stir well to combine, then cover and refrigerate until chilled, about 2 hours.

Fill a cocktail shaker half full with ice and pour in ⅔ cup of the margarita mixture. Shake and strain into two 6-ounce martini glasses. Repeat for the remaining margaritas.

Tasting Notes: Tequilas, Mezcales and Orange Liqueurs

There are a dizzying number of tequilas—nearly 1000 as I'm writing these words—but they're all made by fewer than 150 licensed tequila distilleries in Mexico. Nonetheless, different tequila brands flowing from the same distillery can taste totally unlike one another, depending on the provenance of the agave from which each is made, the style of roasting and fermentation, and, of course, the details of distillation. An exhaustive compendium of tequila tasting notes is beyond the scope of this book, but offering my tasting cheat-sheet is certainly not. I've compiled a list of tequilas (all of them 100% blue agave), mezcales (all from Oaxaca) and orange liqueurs that are widely available in the United States and that represent different regions, price ranges, styles and flavors—all great for crafting cocktails. Each of the tequilas and mezcales is well made and shows off agave's unique flavors. I've chosen them with an eye to value—meaning that the more expensive they are, the more complex and refined they'll taste. Though most of the reposados and añejos in the list are great

for sipping neat, I've actually included them because they shine in a cocktail.

I've given you the prices for 750-ml bottles in 2012 from a large Chicago retailer, simply to give you a perspective on relative prices between brands.

BLANCO TEQUILAS

Jimador blanco ($15.99): bright aroma with eucalyptus, flowers, green bananas and mineral; more sweetness and complexity than you'd expect.

Sauza Blue blanco ($15.99): minty aroma followed by an earthy, gentle sweetness on the palate.

Hornitos blanco ($19.99): alluring mushroom-y earthiness in the nose and softness on the palate.

Milagro blanco ($19.99): beautifully balanced aroma of herbs, flowers, vanilla and mineral; bright, elegant roasty sweetness.

Cazadores blanco ($23.99): wonderfully perfumey with ripe melon and eucalyptus; citrus and buttery vanilla on the palate.

Chinaco blanco ($29.99): salt air and damp

stones in the nose; supple body, gentle sweetness, hints of olive.

Patrón blanco ($33.99): alluring aroma of eucalyptus and olives with soft sweetness that washes over your tongue.

Partida blanco ($34.99): aromas of forest floor; roasty, smooth sweetness on the palate with hints of cinnamon oil.

REPOSADO TEQUILAS

Cuervo Tradicional reposado ($24.99): aromas of pepper, porcini, raw artichoke and almond; flavors of roasted apples, vanilla and nuts.

Gran Centenario reposado ($29.99): aromas of fresh-cut agave from the highlands (mineral, flowers, herbs); elegant richness on the palate with hints of cola (in a good way).

Don Julio reposado ($39.99): a love affair with soft, sweet, roasty agave.

Herradura reposado ($39.99): woodsy, rich aroma with hints of bitter almond; butterscotch and oak on the palate with superlong finish.

Arette reposado ($49.99): elegant nutty nose; baked meringue and coconut on the palate.

AÑEJO TEQUILAS

Corazon añejo ($32.99): cognac-like elegance in the nose with hints of candied lemon peel; wonderful balance between roasted agave, toasted oak and vanilla on the palate.

Tres Generaciones añejo ($39.99): caramelized pineapple, cedar and agave in the nose; raw sugar, sweet spices and beautiful smoothness on the palate. Very long finish.

Oro Azul añejo ($44.99): mineral, roasted coconut, raw sugar, cinnamon and agave in the aroma; symphony of all those aromas on the palate.

El Tesoro añejo ($49.99): flowers and caramelized nuts in the aroma; candied fruit and citrus on the palate.

OAXACAN MEZCALES

Wahaka ($29.99): classic mezcal nose of campfire and citrus; all that on the palate with the volume turned up.

Vida ($39.99): aroma of dessert herbs and citronella; velvety sweet smokiness on the palate with a lovely lingering agave flavor.

Fidencio ($44.99): pears, citrus and a hint of smoke on the nose; luscious fruity sweet agave on the palate.

Chichicapa ($67.99): high-proof nose that hints at prickly pear, plantain, citrus and lilies; complex long-lasting agave sweetness that'll remind you of spicy cinnamon candies.

TRIPLE SEC ORANGE LIQUEURS

DuBouchett Triple Sec (30 proof, $9.99): lively orange marmalade nose; bright orange palate with an attractive bitter orange finish.

Stirrings (30 proof, $13.99): complex nose that unfolds gently into a long-lasting finish.

Bols Orange Curaçao (30 proof, $15.99): burnt sugar and orange peel in the aroma; rich on the palate with a caramelized orange finish.

Cointreau (40 proof, $32.99): the aroma is 100% orange—juice, peel, pith—with light sweetness and long-lasting, clean finish.

BRANDY-BASED ORANGE LIQUEURS

Torres Orange (39 proof, $19.99): delicate perfume of brandy, bitter oranges, toasted almonds and dates; all carry through on the palate with a lovely, balanced sweetness.

Grand Marnier (40 proof, $32.99): Cognac nose and palate infused with complex orange; light on the sweetness, rich on the toasty oakiness.

{ four }

Modern Tequila Cocktails

think we all know that margaritas aren't the only cocktails that can put a spotlight on tequila's beautiful character. Delicious as margaritas are, there are times when that bright citrusy balance isn't what I'm in the mood for.

Maybe I only want to slip a short distance from the iconic margarita balance, toward a gin and tonic, perhaps. Our recipe for Juniper Tequila and Tonic combines a G&T's characteristic spice-infused bitterness with tequila's herbal brightness. You can go simple (just an overnight maceration of juniper berries with tequila, tonic, lime and a shake or two of bitters) or you can tackle making your own tonic (it'll spoil you), even your own bitters. Recipes included.

Then, if you've got that Juniper Tequila around, might as well try the quick-to-assemble Mr. B, a stirred-on-ice fusion of infused tequila, good sweet vermouth and the flavored aperitif wine Cocchi Americano (once you get a bottle, it'll become a new favorite). Our mixologist, Jordan Johnston, put together this unlikely combination, to which, on first sip, I responded, "This is *delicious*—I mean *really, really* delicious!" He christened it Mr. B.

An old-fashioned is about as far from a margarita as you can get—rich and mellow versus tangy and vivid. But when you choose a smooth añejo tequila, splash in a little bourbon, sweeten it up, balance it with bitters and swish around a little ancho chile in the mix, you've got a drink that satisfies both those who love old-fashioneds and those who love aged tequilas and Mexican flavors.

One of the benefits of today's craft cocktail movement is the resurrection of once-popular classics—like El Diablo, the tequila cocktail infused with black currant liqueur (crème de cassis) and ginger ale. The original is great; our version with home-made ginger beer is even better.

No collection of cocktail recipes is complete without a Bloody Mary, sometimes called a Bloody María when made with tequila and chile. Ours is called a Vampiro ("vampire"), and we make it with sangrita, that spicy, tomatoey, citrusy, savory chaser that Mexico serves alongside shots of tequila. Most store-bought sangritas lack freshness and flavor, so I've included a recipe that blends tomato juice with lime, orange, chipotle and Worcestershire.

Right now, I'd have to say that my favorite drink in this whole section is The Bitter Truth, because it combines three things I can't get enough of: tequila, Aperol (the orangey, gentler, kinder Campari) and Cocchi Americano (the delicious, flavored aperitif wine). Shake this triumvirate on ice with a creamy egg white and splash of limeade, garnish it with a sprig of aromatic rosemary and you have a voluptuous cocktail that engages all the senses.

I've left perhaps the most unusual cocktail for last: the Port Sangría. Unusual because it boasts the delicious flavors of sangría while offering the sophistication, punch and balance of a cocktail. Plus, we've offered you two approaches: a ruby port and blanco tequila combo that focuses on fruity refreshment, and a tawny port and añejo tequila one that's richer and nuttier.

Juniper Tequila and Tonic

Bartender's Recipe

BARTENDER'S NOTES: *Okay, there's a lot to this drink the way we make it in the restaurant: infused tequila, homemade tonic, homemade bitters. That's what makes it unique. But don't think you have to tackle the whole thing: a tequila and ordinary tonic is delicious, especially when it's made with juniper-infused tequila. Someday, though, you have to tackle the home- made tonic; it will be a revelation. The same goes for the bitters, which you can use in so many cocktails.*

1½ ounces 100% Juniper Tequila (page 104)

¾ ounce fresh lime juice

3 to 4 drops citrus bitters, store-bought or homemade (we use Lime Bitters, page 88)

3 ounces best-quality tonic water (I like Q tonic)

OR 1 ounce Homemade Tonic Syrup (page 104) plus 2 ounces sparkling water

10 to 15 ice cubes (about 1 cup)

In a 12-ounce Collins glass, combine the Juniper Tequila, lime juice, bitters, tonic (or Tonic Syrup and sparkling water) and ice. Stir well and serve immediately.

Pitcher Recipe for a Party

MAKES 8 COCKTAILS

1½ cups 100% Juniper Tequila (page 104)

¾ cup fresh lime juice

24 to 32 drops (about ½ teaspoon) citrus bit- ters, store-bought or homemade (we use Lime Bitters, page 88)

8 cups ice cubes

3 cups best-quality tonic water (I like Q tonic)

OR 1 cup Homemade Tonic Syrup (page 104) mixed with 2 cups sparkling water

In a pitcher, combine the Juniper Tequila, lime juice and bitters. Cover and refrigerate until chilled, about 2 hours.

Distribute the ice among eight 12-ounce Collins glasses. Pour a generous ¼ cup of the tequila mixture into each glass and stir well. Top each with 3 ounces of the tonic water (or Tonic Syrup and sparkling water) and stir well.

Juniper Tequila

MAKES 2 CUPS

- ¼ cup (¾ ounce) juniper berries
- 2 cups 100% blue agave blanco tequila (see page 95)

Scoop the juniper berries into a glass container and crush them with a cocktail muddler or wooden spoon. Add the tequila, cover and steep for 24 hours.

Strain out the juniper, and the infused tequila is ready to use. Stored in a glass container, it will keep its vibrant flavor for several months.

Homemade Tonic Syrup

MAKES 2 CUPS

- 1¼ cups sugar
- Finely grated zest from 1 lime
- 1½ stalks lemongrass, roughly chopped
- 1 teaspoon cinchona (quinine bark)

In a small saucepan, mix the sugar with 1½ cups water and bring to a boil, stirring until the sugar is completely dissolved. Remove from the heat and add the lime zest, lemongrass and cinchona. Let steep for 20 minutes.

Strain the syrup into a glass container and cool. Cover and store in the refrigerator for up to a month or two.

Mr. B

Bartender's Recipe
MAKES 1 COCKTAIL

BARTENDER'S NOTES: *Since you will be starting your juniper-infused tequila at least a day ahead, I'd suggest chopping a few 2-inch-long strips of orange zest (removed with a vegetable peeler) and adding them to the vermouth to heighten the orange punch.*

1 ounce Juniper Tequila (page 104)

1 ounce sweet vermouth (I love Carpano Antica)

1 ounce Cocchi Americano

6 to 10 ice cubes (about ¾ cup)

A 2-inch strip of orange zest (removed with a vegetable peeler)

In a cocktail shaker, combine the tequila, vermouth, Cocchi Americano and ice. Stir for 10 seconds and strain into a 6-ounce martini glass. Twist the strip of orange zest to release the aromatic oils and float it on top of the cocktail. Serve immediately.

Pitcher Recipe for a Party
MAKES 8 COCKTAILS

1 cup Juniper Tequila (page 104)

1 cup sweet vermouth (I love Carpano Antica)

1 cup Cocchi Americano

6 cups ice cubes

Eight 2-inch strips of orange zest (removed with a vegetable peeler)

In a pitcher, combine the tequila, vermouth and Cocchi Americano. Cover and refrigerate until chilled, about 2 hours.

Fill a cocktail shaker half full with ice and pour in ¼ cup of the tequila mixture. Stir for 10 seconds and strain into two martini glasses. Repeat for the remaining cocktails. Garnish with the orange zest.

Tequila Old-Fashioned

Bartender's Recipe

MAKES 1 COCKTAIL

BARTENDER'S NOTES: *You might not believe it, but ancho chile has a lot in common with bourbon and añejo tequila: (1) ancho's deep richness echoes the complexity of both aged spirits, (2) the chile's natural smokiness walks hand-in-hand with what you taste from the liquors' toasted-barrel aging, and (3) ancho's gentle spiciness, though a different sensation, has something in common with alcohol's customary ardor.*

Purist fans of bourbon and añejo tequila will probably be horrified by my combining them here. To them I say, just try it. This drink is remarkably delicious.

Orange bitters are best here, but Angostura or Peychaud make a good drink too.

1 dried ancho chile, stemmed and seeded

1 ounce 100% blue agave añejo tequila (see page 96)

1 ounce bourbon (the better the bourbon, the better the drink will be—Four Roses is a delicious, value-conscious choice for a small-batch bourbon)

3 drops orange bitters, store-bought or homemade (page 88)

¼ ounce agave syrup (raw organic syrup gives the best flavor) or Rich Simple Syrup (page 21)

6 to 10 ice cubes (about ¾ cup)

Cut a piece of chile that's roughly 1 x 2 inches, scoop it into a cocktail shaker and muddle it with a cocktail muddler or a wooden spoon until it is noticeably more aromatic (it won't break apart). Pour in the tequila, bourbon, bitters and agave or simple syrup. Scoop in the ice and stir for 10 seconds. Strain into a 10-ounce rocks glass. Retrieve the piece of chile and float it on top. Serve immediately.

Pitcher Recipe for a Party

MAKES 8 COCKTAILS

1 cup 100% blue agave añejo tequila (see page 96)

1 cup bourbon (the better the bourbon, the better this drink will be—Four Roses is a delicious value-conscious choice for a small-batch bourbon)

24 drops orange bitters, store-bought or homemade (page 88)

¼ cup agave syrup (raw organic syrup gives the best flavor) or Rich Simple Syrup (page 21)

2 dried ancho chiles, stemmed and seeded

6 cups ice cubes

In a pitcher, combine the tequila, bourbon, bitters and agave or simple syrup. Cover and refrigerate until chilled, about 2 hours.

Cut the chiles into 8 equal-size pieces, roughly 1 x 2 inches.

Scoop 2 pieces of chile into a cocktail shaker and muddle with a cocktail muddler or a wooden spoon until they are noticeably more aromatic (they won't break apart). Fill the cocktail shaker half full with ice, pour in a generous ½ cup of the tequila-bourbon mixture and stir for 10 seconds. Strain into two 10-ounce rocks glasses. Fish out the chile pieces and float one on top of each cocktail. Repeat for the remaining cocktails.

Mexican El Diablo

Bartender's Recipe

MAKES 1 COCKTAIL

BARTENDER'S NOTES: *Though you could easily make this cocktail with ginger beer or ginger ale, the homemade ginger beer is really delicious and simple—well,* simple *if the ingredients are easily available. The simplest incarnation of Ginger Beer Syrup is the simple combination of water, sugar and ginger (in that case, increase the ginger to 1/3 cup). But lemongrass (available in well-stocked or specialty grocery stores) adds a citrusy, floral note, while cinchona bark (available online) adds an appealing bitterness. To change things up, we occasionally substitute framboise (raspberry) or Fragoli liqueur (strawberry) for the Diablo's traditional crème de cassis (black currant).*

1½ ounces 100% blue agave resposado tequila (see page 96)

¾ ounce fresh lime juice

½ ounce crème de cassis (black currant liqueur—we use Jules Theuriet brand)

1 ounce Homemade Ginger Beer Syrup (page 112)

1 ounce sparkling water

10 to 15 ice cubes (about 1 cup)

A 2-inch strip of lime zest (removed with a vegetable peeler)

Pour the tequila, lime juice, crème de cassis and Homemade Ginger Beer Syrup into a 10-ounce rocks glass. Add the sparkling water and ice and stir for about 15 seconds. Twist the strip of lime zest to release the aromatic oils and nestle it into the cocktail. Serve immediately.

Pitcher Recipe for a Party

MAKES 8 COCKTAILS

1½ cups 100% blue agave resposado tequila (see page 96)

¾ cup fresh lime juice

½ cup crème de cassis (black currant liqueur— we use Jules Theuriet brand)

1 cup Homemade Ginger Beer Syrup (page 112)

8 ounces sparkling water

8 cups ice cubes

Eight 2-inch strips of lime zest (removed with a vegetable peeler)

In a pitcher, combine the tequila, lime juice, crème de cassis and Homemade Ginger Beer Syrup. Stir well, cover and refrigerate until chilled, about 2 hours

Pour a scant ½ cup of the tequila mixture into each of eight 10-ounce rocks glasses. Top each with 1 ounce of the sparkling water and a cup of ice. Twist the strips of lime zest to release the aromatic oils and add one to each cocktail.

<<< Mexican El Diablo (page 109)

Homemade
Ginger Beer Syrup

MAKES 2 CUPS

- 1¼ cups (9 ounces) sugar
- ¼ cup (1 ounce) minced ginger (no need to peel)
- 2 tablespoons (½ ounce) chopped lemongrass (you'll need about ⅓ stalk of lemongrass)
- 1 teaspoon cinchona (quinine bark)
- ¼ cup plus 2 tablespoons fresh lime juice

In a small saucepan, mix the sugar with 1½ cups water and bring to a boil. Simmer briskly over medium heat, stirring regularly, until the sugar is completely dissolved. Remove from the heat and add the ginger, lemongrass and cinchona, Cover and let steep for 1 hour.

Strain the syrup into a glass container. Add the lime juice. Cover and store in the refrigerator for up to several weeks.

Vampiro

Bartender's Recipe

MAKES 1 COCKTAIL

BARTENDER'S NOTES: *To make Chipotle Salt, mix equal parts powdered chipotle chile and coarse (kosher) salt. If you think these proportions may yield a salt that's on the spicy side for your guests, salt just half the rim of each glass.*

Many people know sangrita only from the bottled stuff, most of which tastes like a pasteurized, orangey, spicy, slightly sweet, thinned-out tomato juice. It certainly doesn't taste fresh. That's why I've included the recipe we use at the Frontera bar.

Chipotle Salt (see Bartender's Notes) or coarse
   (kosher) salt (optional)

1 lime wedge (optional)

2 rounds of unpeeled cucumber

1½ ounces 100% blue agave blanco tequila (see
   page 95)

4 ounces Homemade Sangrita (page 116)

6 to 10 ice cubes (about ¾ cup)

1 fresh cilantro sprig (optional)

If using, spread the Chipotle Salt or coarse salt on a small plate. Moisten the rim of a 10-ounce highball glass with the lime wedge and upend the glass onto the salt to coat the rim.

Muddle 1 cucumber round with a cocktail muddler or a wooden spoon in the bottom of the prepared glass until roughly mashed. Pour in the tequila and Sangrita and stir to combine. Scoop in the ice and stir again. Cut a slit halfway into the remaining cucumber round and use it to garnish the rim of the glass— a sprig of cilantro stuck into the cucumber wheel is a nice touch.

Pitcher Recipe for a Party

MAKES 8 COCKTAILS

16 rounds unpeeled cucumber

1½ cups 100% blue agave blanco tequila (see page 95)

4 cups Homemade Sangrita (page 116)

1 lime wedge (optional)

Chipotle Salt (see Bartender's Notes) or coarse (kosher) salt (optional)

6 cups ice cubes

8 fresh cilantro sprigs (optional)

In the bottom of a pitcher, muddle 8 cucumber rounds with a cocktail muddler or wooden spoon until coarsely mashed. Add the tequila and Sangrita and stir. Cover and refrigerate until chilled, about 2 hours.

If desired, use the lime and Chipotle Salt to crust the rims of eight 10-ounce highball glasses as described in the Bartender's Recipe. Distribute the ice among the prepared glasses. Pour ⅔ cup of the tequila-Sangrita mixture into each glass and stir. Garnish each glass with a cucumber round, and the cilantro sprigs if you wish.

Homemade Sangrita

MAKES ABOUT 4 CUPS

- 2 cups good-quality tomato juice
- ⅔ cup fresh lime juice
- 1 cup fresh orange juice
- 2 small canned chipotle chiles, finely chopped, with some of the adobo canning sauce (a heaping tablespoon total)
- 1 teaspoon black pepper, preferably freshly ground
- A generous ½ teaspoon salt
- 1 tablespoon plus 1 teaspoon Worcestershire sauce

Mix all the ingredients together in a glass container. Cover and refrigerate. Use within a few days for the freshest flavor.

The Bitter Truth

Bartender's Recipe

MAKES 1 COCKTAIL

BARTENDER'S NOTES: *This is a very modern cocktail featuring two very popular and delicious aperitifs from Italy: Aperol (think of it as an orangey Campari-lite) and Cocchi Americano (made from Moscato d'Asti). Both have found a permanent home in my libations cabinet, Aperol being featured in my favorite brunch drink (orange juice, sparkling wine and Aperol) and Cocchi Americano having become a favorite to sip in front of the fireplace.*

ABOUT USING RAW EGG WHITES: *A few years ago, Jason White wrote in a* Washington Post *article that you are four times more likely to choke on a handful of bar nuts than to get salmonella from eggs. Yet the dreaded salmonella is what keeps most people from using raw egg whites in mayonnaise and mousse and, of course, to create that great cocktail luxury: inimitably creamy froth floating atop a delicious libation. Truth is, you can assuage any concerns by buying a container of pasteurized egg whites (they're available in most grocery stores these days). Or do what I do and buy eggs from a local cage-free grower: smaller production is often done with greater care and passion.*

1 egg (or 1 ounce pasteurized egg whites)

1 ounce 100% blue agave reposado tequila (see page 96)

2 ounces *Limonada* (page 21)

1 ounce Cocchi Americano

1 ounce Aperol

6 to 10 ice cubes (about ¾ cup)

1 fresh rosemary sprig

Crack the egg and cup the yolk in one half of the shell while letting the white fall into a cocktail shaker, or measure 1 ounce of pasteurized egg whites into your shaker. (Save the yolk to use in flan, mayonnaise, ice cream or such.) Cover and shake for 15 seconds, until the egg white is frothy. Add the tequila, *Limonada*, Cocchi Americano, Aperol and ice. Cover and shake vigorously until frothy and cold; tiny ice crystals will appear in the drink after about 15 seconds of shaking.

Rub the sprig of rosemary around the rim of a 10-ounce rocks glass. Strain the cocktail into the glass and garnish with the rosemary. Serve immediately.

Pitcher Recipe for a Party
MAKES 8 COCKTAILS

1 cup 100% blue agave reposado tequila (see page 96)

2 cups *Limonada* (1 cup fresh lime juice mixed with ½ cup sugar and 1½ cups water will yield 2⅔ cups. Dilute the leftover *Limonada* with a little sparkling water for a refreshing limeade while you are preparing for your party.)

1 cup Cocchi Americano

1 cup Aperol

8 eggs (or 8 ounces pasteurized egg whites)

6 cups ice cubes

8 fresh rosemary sprigs

In a pitcher, combine the tequila, *Limonada*, Cocchi Americano and Aperol. Cover and refrigerate until chilled, about 2 hours.

One by one, crack 2 of the eggs and cup the yolk in one half of the shell while letting the white fall into a cocktail shaker, or measure 2 ounces of the pasteurized egg whites into your shaker. Cover and shake for 15 seconds, or until the egg whites are frothy. Fill the shaker half full with ice and pour in a scant 1¼ cups of the tequila mixture. Shake and strain into two 10-ounce rocks glasses. Repeat for the remaining cocktails. Rub a sprig of rosemary around the rim of each glass, then garnish with the sprig.

Port Sangría

Bartender's Recipe

MAKES 1 COCKTAIL

BARTENDER'S NOTES: *When you make this unexpectedly tasty drink with ruby port and blanco tequila, I think you'll concur that it qualifies as what I'd call a "sipping sangría"— not the quaffable sangría classic, but more complex, more satisfying. Made with tawny port and añejo, the flavors are deeper, blossoming with nuttiness and depth. Though featuring port may lead you to think the drink will be sweet, the palate never perceives it that way. Serve it before dinner, not after.*

1½ ounces 100% blue agave blanco tequila (see page 95) if using ruby port

    OR 1½ ounces 100% blue agave añejo tequila (see page 96) if using tawny port

2 ounces *Limonada* (page 21)

½ ounce Cointreau

1 ounce ruby port (we like Niepoort)

    OR 1 ounce tawny port (we like Niepoort)

6 to 10 ice cubes (about ¾ cup)

In a cocktail shaker, combine the tequila, *Limonada*, Cointreau, port and ice. Cover and shake vigorously until frothy and cold; tiny ice crystals will appear in the drink after about 15 seconds of shaking. Strain into a 10-ounce rocks glass and serve immediately.

Pitcher Recipe for a Party

MAKES 8 COCKTAILS

1½ cups 100% blue agave blanco tequila (see page 95) if using ruby port

    OR 1½ cups 100% blue agave añejo tequila (see page 96) if using tawny port

2 cups *Limonada* (1 cup fresh lime juice mixed with ½ cup sugar and 1½ cups water will yield 2⅔ cups, a little more than you need. Add some sparkling water to the leftover to make a delicious sparkling limeade.)

½ cup Cointreau

1 cup ruby port (we like Niepoort)

    OR 1 cup tawny port (we like Niepoort)

6 cups ice cubes

In a pitcher, combine the tequila, *Limonada*, Cointreau and port. Cover and refrigerate until chilled, about 2 hours.

Fill a cocktail shaker half full with ice and pour in 1¼ cups of the cocktail mixture. Shake and strain into two 10-ounce rocks glasses. Repeat for the remaining cocktails.

{ five }

Agua Fresca
Cocktails

guas frescas are Mexico's original soft drinks. They're not effervescent, not dark and syrupy and, for the most part, not artificially flavored. They are just lively refreshment, mostly made from fresh fruit, lime, sugar and water (plus, occasionally, certain vegetables and herbs), and the best ones show a nice balance of tangy and sweet. At Frontera, for much of the year, we have a standard rotation of daily-changing *aguas frescas*. And each day we are open (Tuesday through Saturday) we transform the *agua fresca* into a cocktail. They're very adaptable that way.

The easiest way to turn these drinks from "soft" to "hard" is to add a shot of blanco tequila or white rum. Delicious to be sure, but we've decided to take them to the next level, turning each *agua fresca* into a full-fledged cocktail.

Come into Frontera, Topolobampo or Xoco on most Tuesdays, and an amber, resonant blend of rich apple cider and bright tamarind will be filling icy glasses. Embellish it with tequila, blood orange liqueur (or triple sec), Calvados and lime, serve it in a tall glass crusted with spiced salt, and delicious refreshment transforms into the stuff of memory.

Perhaps the most refreshing *agua fresca* of the week shows up on Wednesday, and, for some neophytes, it requires more convincing than others. A blend of cucumber, lime and mint, it's revitalizing in a honeydew-melon sort of way. But with a spark of fresh ginger, ginger liqueur and a good douse of blanco tequila, the pale green libation becomes the perfect cocktail when barbecuing on a hot summer afternoon or to sip with spicy snacks at any time of year.

Starting about midsummer, our Thursday offering is a classic watermelon *agua fresca*—one of the simplest and most delicious *aguas frescas* you can make. Watermelon gets blended with a little lime, a little sugar and water. Great watermelon means a great *agua fresca*. Stir in the brightness of an unaged tequila and the alluring orangey bitterness of Aperol, and you've got a cocktail that tastes amazing—and anything but simple.

Though Chicago doesn't have the climate for growing passion fruit, these are regularly in the market during the late summer and early fall. And their mesmerizing tropical aroma stars in another of our favorite *aguas frescas*, one that we pair with orange and serve on Fridays. You can serve it any time of the year if you use the frozen passion fruit puree available in Mexican groceries (Goya brand is decent), specialty stores or online; I haven't found a bottled or canned passion fruit that I've liked as well in the *agua fresca*. When we transform that beautiful, sunny beverage into a cocktail, we do it simply: just a little energy from tequila and lime, mellowed by Cointreau.

From morning to night, Saturdays always seem to have an air of celebration at Frontera. While the cucumber-mint and watermelon-lime *aguas frescas* seem like wonderful workday refreshment, Coconut *Horchata*, our luxurious take on that milky-cinnamony Mexican classic, is pure weekend pleasure.

Horchata is typically a blended drink of raw rice, cinnamon and sugar (most people add a little milk to give it body), but this version borrows the best from many regional specialties. We use toasted almonds (as they do in Oaxaca) to give it nuttiness, coconut (as they do in Yucatan) for tropical richness, and a little sweetened condensed milk (that Mexican favorite) for a unique carameliness. All in all, it's the best *horchata* I've ever tasted. You could simply add a splash of rum and call it a cocktail (very good, by the way), but when you add orange juice, triple sec and tequila, you've got an adult, tropical Dreamsicle of a drink that is totally seductive.

Apple-Tamarind Cocktail
(Tuesday)
Bartender's Recipe

MAKES 8 COCKTAILS

BARTENDER'S NOTES: *Pür Likör Spice Blood Orange Liqueur is pretty amazing stuff (and adds incredible dynamism to this cocktail), but it may not be within everyone's easy reach. That said, the cocktail is very good with triple sec too. The Tamarind Puree you'll need for making the Tamarind Cider* Agua Fresca *can vary a lot in strength and quality. Read the notes before the Tamarind Puree recipe on page 84.*

To make Spiced Salt for crusting the glasses, mix ¼ cup each coarse (kosher) salt and sugar, with 1 tablespoon coarsely ground allspice.

To make a single cocktail, combine 4 ounces Tamarind Cider Agua Fresca, *1½ ounces blanco tequila, ¼ ounce fresh lime juice, ½ ounce Calvados, ½ ounce blood orange liqueur or triple sec and ¼ ounce agave or Rich Simple Syrup (page 21) in a 12-ounce highball glass crusted with spiced salt. Stir, fill with about 1 cup of ice and serve.*

If you'd like to offer both "soft" and "hard" variations, simply make double the agua fresca *recipe, use half for the cocktail preparation and serve the rest over ice in tall glasses.*

FOR 4 CUPS TAMARIND CIDER *AGUA FRESCA*

2 cups Tamarind Puree (page 84)

1½ cups apple cider

½ cup sugar

FOR TURNING THE *AGUA FRESCA* INTO COCKTAILS

1½ cups 100% blue agave blanco tequila (see page 95)

¼ cup fresh lime juice

½ cup Calvados

½ cup Pür Likör Spice Blood Orange Liqueur or triple sec

¼ cup agave syrup (light organic syrup gives the best flavor) or Rich Simple Syrup (page 21)

Spiced Salt (see Bartender's Notes) or a 50-50 mix of salt and sugar

1 lime wedge

8 cups ice cubes

Make the **agua fresca***:* In a large pitcher, combine the tamarind puree, apple cider, sugar and ½ cup water. Stir well. (This mixture can be covered and refrigerated for up to 3 days.)

From **agua fresca** *to cocktails:* To the pitcher of *agua fresca*, add the tequila, lime juice, Calvados, blood orange liqueur or triple sec and agave or simple syrup. Stir well to combine, then cover and refrigerate until chilled, about 2 hours.

Spread the Spiced Salt on a small plate. Moisten the rims of eight 12-ounce highball glasses with the lime wedge and upend the glasses onto the salt to crust the rims. Fill each glass with about 1 cup of ice, then pour in a scant cup of the cocktail mixture. The drink is ready to carry to your guests.

Tangy Cucumber-Mint Cocktail

(Wednesday)

MAKES 8 COCKTAILS

BARTENDER'S NOTES: *Muddling all that ginger may be more than you want to tackle. An easy alternative is to put it into a freezer bag and mash it with a rolling pin or meat mallet; you'll want to use a little extra in that case, because it's hard to get all of the mashed ginger and its juice out of the bag and into the pitcher. Or use a food processor (one of those little ones, if you have it) to chop the ginger to a coarse puree.*

Sometimes I like to muddle additional mint leaves with the ginger for a stronger herbal punch. No Domaine de Canton? You can make a good cocktail without it by just increasing the tequila to 2 cups. I'd increase the ginger too. And you'll likely think that the finished drink needs a little extra sweetening: use agave syrup or Rich Simple Syrup (page 21).

To make a single cocktail, muddle 1 slice of ginger in a 12-ounce highball glass. Add 4 ounces Tangy Cucumber-Mint Agua Fresca, *1½ ounces blanco tequila, ½ ounce ginger liqueur and 1 ounce sparkling water. Fill with about 1 cup of ice, stir, garnish with a lime wedge and serve.*

If you'd like to offer both "soft" and "hard" variations, simply make double the agua fresca *recipe, use half for the cocktail preparation and serve the rest over ice in tall glasses.*

FOR 4 CUPS TANGY CUCUMBER-MINT *AGUA FRESCA*

4 to 5 fresh mint sprigs (½ ounce)

1 large (8-ounce) cucumber, peeled and roughly chopped

½ cup fresh lime juice

½ cup sugar

FOR TURNING THE *AGUA FRESCA* INTO COCKTAILS

8 slices peeled ginger the thickness of a quarter

1½ cups 100% blue agave blanco tequila (see page 95)

½ cup Domaine de Canton ginger liqueur

About 8 cups ice cubes

1 cup sparkling water

1 lime, cut into 8 wedges

Make the **agua fresca***:* Strip the leaves from the mint stalks. In a blender, combine the mint leaves, cucumber, lime juice, sugar and 2 cups water. Blend on high until smooth. Look at the measurements on the side of your blender jar and add enough water to bring the quantity to 4 cups. Strain to remove any seeds or unblended bits. Pour into a storage container, cover and refrigerate until you are ready to use—which should be within a few hours for the freshest flavor and look.

From **agua fresca** *to cocktails:* In the bottom of a large pitcher, muddle the ginger with a cocktail muddler or wooden spoon until you have a coarse mash. Add the tequila, ginger liqueur and Tangy Cucumber-Mint *Agua Fresca*. Stir, cover and refrigerate until chilled, about 2 hours.

Fill eight 12-ounce highball glasses with about a cup of ice each. Pour ¾ cup of the cocktail mixture into each glass, making sure to get some of the muddled ginger in each one. Top each glass with an ounce of sparkling water and stir with a long-handled bar spoon. Garnish each glass with a lime wedge and carry to your guests.

Watermelon Cocktail

(Thursday)

Bartender's Recipe

MAKES 8 COCKTAILS

BARTENDER'S NOTES: *If you have a watermelon with seeds, pulse it in the blender with the other ingredients until the flesh is broken up and the seeds are dislodged. Strain, return to the blender jar and blend until smooth.*

To make a single cocktail, mix 4 ounces Watermelon-Lime Agua Fresca with 1½ ounces blanco tequila and ¾ ounce Aperol in a 12-ounce highball glass. Fill with about 1 cup of ice cubes, stir and serve.

If you'd like to offer both "soft" and "hard" variations, simply make double the agua fresca recipe, use half for the cocktail preparation and serve the rest over ice in tall glasses.

FOR 4 CUPS WATERMELON-LIME *AGUA FRESCA*

A 3-pound chunk of ripe seedless watermelon

½ cup fresh lime juice

½ cup sugar

FOR TURNING THE *AGUA FRESCA* INTO COCKTAILS

1½ cups 100% blue agave blanco tequila (see page 95)

¾ cup Aperol

8 cups ice cubes

Make the agua fresca: Cut the rind off the watermelon, then cut the fruit into rough 1-inch chunks; you need about a generous 4 cups (1½ pounds) cleaned cubes. Scoop into a blender, add the lime juice and sugar and blend until smooth. Look at the measurements on the side of your blender jar and add enough water to bring the quantity to 4 cups. Strain to remove any seeds and unblended bits. Pour into a storage container, cover and refrigerate; the *agua fresca* is best used the same day it is made.

From agua fresca to cocktails: In a large pitcher, combine the tequila, Aperol and Watermelon-Lime *Agua Fresca*. Stir well to combine, then cover and refrigerate until chilled, about 2 hours.

Pour about ¾ cup of the cocktail mixture into each of eight 12-ounce highball glasses. Add about a cup of ice to each one and serve immediately.

Orange-Passion Fruit Cocktail
(Friday)
Bartender's Recipe

MAKES 8 COCKTAILS

BARTENDER'S NOTES: *When you see fresh passion fruit in the market, it will usually be one of two varieties: the small purple variety (its leathery skin looks a little shriveled when the fruit is ripe) or the large yellow variety that looks like a really small melon.*

To make Star Anise Salt for crusting the glasses, mix equal parts coarse (kosher) salt and coarsely ground star anise.

To make a single cocktail, mix 4 ounces Orange-Passion Fruit Agua Fresca *with 1½ ounces blanco tequila, ½ ounce fresh lime juice and ½ ounce Cointreau in a 12-ounce highball glass and add about a cup of ice. Garnish with star anise if you wish.*

If you'd like to offer both "soft" and "hard" variations, simply make double the agua fresca *recipe, use half for the cocktail preparation and serve the rest over ice in tall glasses.*

FOR 4 CUPS ORANGE-PASSION FRUIT
AGUA FRESCA

A generous ½ cup fresh passion fruit pulp
(you'll need about 3 large yellow or 6 small
purple fruits—halve and scrape out the seedy
pulp)
OR 1 cup frozen passion fruit pulp

2 cups fresh orange juice

A generous ½ cup sugar

FOR TURNING THE *AGUA FRESCA* INTO
COCKTAILS

1½ cups 100% blue agave blanco tequila (see
page 95)

½ cup fresh lime juice

½ cup Cointreau or triple sec

Star Anise Salt (see Bartender's Notes) or
coarse (kosher) salt

1 lime wedge

8 cups ice cubes

8 whole star anise for garnish (optional)

Make the agua fresca: *If using fresh passion fruit*, scoop it into a blender with the orange juice and sugar. Pulse 5 or 6 times to dislodge the seeds from the pulp (but not to break up the seeds), then pour the mixture through a medium-mesh strainer into a bowl. Discard the seeds, return the mixture to the blender and process until all the sugar is dissolved. Add enough water to bring the quantity to 4 cups. Pour into a storage container.

If using frozen passion fruit pulp, in a storage container, whisk together the passion fruit pulp, orange juice and sugar until the sugar is dissolved. Stir in ¾ cup water.

Cover and refrigerate; the *agua fresca* is best used within a couple of days.

From agua fresca *to cocktails:* In a pitcher, combine the tequila, lime juice, Cointreau or triple sec and Orange–Passion Fruit *Agua Fresca*. Stir well to combine, then cover and refrigerate until chilled, about 2 hours.

Spread the Star Anise Salt or coarse salt on a small plate. Moisten the rims of eight 12-ounce highball glasses with the lime wedge and upend the glasses onto the salt to crust the rims. Pour a generous ¾ cup of the tequila mixture into each crusted glass and add about 1 cup of ice. Top each drink with a star anise if you wish, and carry to your guests.

Orange-Passion Fruit Cocktail (page 133) >>>

Coconut *Horchata* Cocktail

(Saturday)

MAKES 8 COCKTAILS

BARTENDER'S NOTES: *This* horchata *isn't hard to make, though it probably includes a few ingredients you don't have in your cupboard. If rice flour can't be found in your local super-market, it's available in most Mexican and Asian groceries and online.*

I find it hard to divide a can of coconut milk, simply because the fat is typically congealed on top of the watery-looking liquid below. To get an even distribution of both fat and liquid, scrape the entire can of coconut milk into your blender, blend until smooth and pour it into a pitcher. Measure the amount you need, return it to the blender and continue.

The sweetened condensed milk—a common ingredient in Mexico—gives this horchata *a distinctive richness with caramel overtones. If you don't have it (or don't want to open a can just for 3 tablespoons), you can make a delicious drink without it; you'll need to add another 2 tablespoons sugar and 1 tablespoon milk.*

To make a single cocktail, mix 2 ounces Coconut Horchata *with 1½ ounces blanco tequila, ½ ounce triple sec and 2 ounces fresh orange juice in a 12-ounce highball glass and add about 1 cup of ice.*

FOR 4 CUPS COCONUT *HORCHATA*

Scant ¼ cup (1 ounce) skinless whole almonds

Half a 14-ounce can (¾ cup plus 2 tablespoons) of coconut milk (see Bartender's Notes)

3 tablespoons sweetened condensed milk

¾ cup whole milk

2 tablespoons rice flour

¼ teaspoon ground cinnamon (preferably Mexican *canela*)

1½ teaspoons pure vanilla extract

½ cup sugar

FOR TURNING THE *HORCHATA* INTO COCKTAILS

1½ cups 100% blue agave blanco tequila (see page 95)

½ cup triple sec

2 cups fresh orange juice

8 cups ice cubes

To make the Coconut Horchata: Turn on the oven to 325 degrees. Spread the almonds on a baking sheet. Place in the oven for 8 minutes, or until they are lightly toasted. Cool.

In a blender jar, combine the coconut milk, sweetened condensed milk, whole milk, rice flour, cinnamon, vanilla, sugar and toasted almonds. Add 2 cups water and blend until the mixture feels only the slightest bit gritty when a drop is rubbed between your fingers. Strain through a fine-mesh sieve. (If yours isn't fine, line it with a couple of layers of dampened cheesecloth.) Stir in more water if needed to bring the volume up to 4 cups.

The *horchata* will taste fresh for several days if it is stored covered in the refrigerator.

From horchata to cocktails: In a large pitcher, combine the tequila, triple sec, orange juice and 2 cups of the Coconut *Horchata* (save the rest of the *horchata* for another batch or serve it to those who prefer a nonalcoholic drink). Stir well to combine, then cover and refrigerate until chilled, about 2 hours.

Pour about ¾ cup of the cocktail mixture into each of eight 12-ounce highball glasses. Add about a cup of ice to each glass and serve immediately.

{ six }

Tequila Dessert Cocktails

There are special times and places for dessert cocktails. At my house, one comes along about midsummer, when I've collected some friends in the backyard. We've feasted on simple freshness from the farmers' market, most of which has had a tour across my grill and been served with glasses of dry rosé. And then there's dessert: it could be ice cream or sorbet, but to me that never sounds as exciting as sharing a bowl of perfectly ripe, locally grown peaches and sipping a creamy Café Tacuba.

The Café Tacuba is the first dessert cocktail we put on our menu at Frontera and Topolobampo and it's still my go-to: coffee, Kahlúa, half-and-half and blanco tequila shaken with ice until frothy and served in a glass crusted with Mexican chocolate. Nearly as perfect as a dessert cocktail (or cocktail for dessert) can be.

I could really say all the same things about the Caramel Apple Cocktail, though I'd serve it for dessert after a meal that celebrates local fall bounty—and the great fresh cider we get in the Midwest. The other star ingredient, of course, is the *cajeta* or *dulce de leche*. Store-bought is easy, but really no easier than the 24-hour slow-cooker version I developed for this book: stir milk, sugar and cinnamon together in the slow-cooker, let cook for 24 hours and enjoy the amazing, traditional flavor of *cajeta*. So much richer and more complex than caramel sauce.

When you're in Oaxaca, the rustic local chocolate is so freshly ground that it still has all its bright flavors and tangy acidity—most of which has disappeared in the smooth chocolate truffles and such we're used to. Oaxacan chocolate is so flavorful, in fact, that it's most commonly turned into a warm beverage with only the addition of steaming-hot water. Our Cinnamon Chocolate Cocktail captures that Oaxacan experience by brightening chocolate sauce with blanco tequila, filling in the cracks with crème de cacao and perfuming the whole experience, in typical Mexican fashion, with cinnamon. Hopefully you'll lay your hands on the tender-flaky sticks of true cinnamon called *canela* (available in most ethnic markets). It's wonderfully floral and spicy at the same time.

The Coconut-Vanilla *Horchata* Cocktail is just plain luxury: rich and creamy, tropical and delicious. This is the kind of dessert cocktail I think of for those other perfect dessert cocktail moments, the times when it's pure celebration, the commemoration of a special moment, holiday, anniversary, occasion, birthday. Sipping this cocktail will heap one unforgettable moment on another.

Café Tacuba

Bartender's Recipe

MAKES 1 COCKTAIL

BARTENDER'S NOTES: *To prepare the chocolate for rimming the glass, roughly chop some Mexican chocolate, then pulverize it in a food processor or an electric spice grinder. Ibarra and Abuelita are brands of Mexican chocolate commonly found in well-stocked groceries—Mexican or otherwise—but specialty brands like Taza will give you much more chocolate flavor. You may think it odd that I've called for a blanco tequila here, as aged spirits, after all, are associated with after-dinner libations. The blanco's brightness makes this drink sparkle.*

Finely ground Mexican chocolate (See Bartender's Notes)

1 ounce 100% blue agave blanco tequila (see page 95)

1 ounce Kahlúa

1 ounce espresso or very strong coffee, at room temperature

1 ounce half-and-half

6 to 10 ice cubes (about ¾ cup)

Spread the ground chocolate on a small plate. Moisten the rim of a 6-ounce martini glass with a wet paper towel, then upend the glass onto the chocolate to crust the rim.

In a cocktail shaker, combine the tequila, Kahlúa, espresso or strong coffee, half-and-half and ice. Cover and shake vigorously until frothy and cold; tiny ice crystals will appear in the drink after about 15 seconds of shaking. Strain into the chocolate-crusted glass and serve immediately.

Pitcher Recipe for a Party

MAKES 8 COCKTAILS

1 cup 100% blue agave blanco tequila (see page 95)

1 cup Kahlúa

1 cup espresso or very strong coffee, at room temperature

1 cup half-and-half

Finely ground Mexican chocolate (see Bartender's Notes)

6 cups ice cubes

In a pitcher, combine the tequila, Kahlúa, espresso or strong coffee, and half-and-half. Cover and refrigerate until chilled, about 2 hours.

Crust the rims of eight 6-ounce martini glasses with ground chocolate as described in the Bartender's Recipe. Fill a cocktail shaker half full with ice and pour in 1 cup of the cocktail mixture. Shake and strain into two of the prepared glasses. Repeat for the remaining cocktails.

Caramel Apple Cocktail

Bartender's Recipe

MAKES 1 COCKTAIL

BARTENDER'S NOTES: Cajeta, *that adored, long-simmered caramely milk confection that goes by the name* dulce de leche *in non-Mexican parts of Latin America, is the cornerstone of this drink. You have options. You can make your own—it takes a little time, but the ingredients are easy and my slow-cooker version is foolproof. In Mexico,* cajeta *is often made from goat's milk. Funky goatiness isn't what you're looking for in this cocktail, so if you make your own or buy* cajeta, *choose cow's milk, not goat's.* Dulce de leche *is almost always a bovine product. Caramel sauce is very good in this cocktail, but not as distinctive as* cajeta.

1½ ounces 100% blue agave blanco tequila (see page 95)

½ ounce *cajeta* (store-bought or homemade, page 147), *dulce de leche* or top-quality caramel sauce, at room temperature

1½ ounces apple cider (preferably an unpasteurized one from the farmers' market)

½ ounce Calvados

6 to 10 ice cubes (about ¾ cup)

In a cocktail shaker, combine the tequila, *cajeta, dulce de leche* or caramel sauce, cider, Calvados and ice. Cover and shake vigorously until frothy and cold; tiny ice crystals will appear in the drink after about 15 seconds of shaking. Strain into a 6-ounce martini glass and serve immediately.

Pitcher Recipe for a Party
MAKES 8 COCKTAILS

1½ cups 100% blue agave blanco tequila (see page 95)

½ cup *cajeta* (store-bought or homemade, page 147), *dulce de leche* or top-quality caramel sauce, at room temperature

1½ cups apple cider (preferably an unpasteurized one from the farmers' market)

½ cup Calvados

6 cups ice

In a pitcher, combine the tequila, *cajeta*, *dulce de leche* or caramel sauce, cider and Calvados. Cover and refrigerate until chilled, about 2 hours.

Fill a cocktail shaker half full with ice and pour in 1 cup of the cocktail mixture. Shake and strain into two 6-ounce martini glasses. Repeat for the remaining cocktails.

Twenty-Four-Hour *Cajeta*

MAKES ABOUT 3 CUPS

- 2 quarts milk (cow's milk or half cow's milk, half goat's milk)
- 2 cups sugar
- A 3-inch piece of cinnamon stick (preferably Mexican *canela*)
- ½ teaspoon baking soda, dissolved in 1 tablespoon water

Pour the milk into a slow-cooker. Whisk in the sugar. Add the cinnamon and dissolved baking soda and stir well. Turn the slow-cooker on high and cook, *uncovered*, for about 24 hours. After about 18 hours or so, the *cajeta* will have darkened to light golden brown. That's when to begin keeping an eye on it. Stir it from time to time to make sure it's cooking evenly. When it is noticeably thick and richly golden, test a couple of drops on a cold plate. The cooled *cajeta* should be the consistency of caramel sauce. If yours is still a little runny, let it cook longer.

When your *cajeta* is ready, strain it through a fine-mesh strainer into a bowl or wide-mouth storage jar. It will keep for a month or more covered in the refrigerator.

Cinnamon Chocolate Cocktail

Bartender's Recipe

MAKES 1 COCKTAIL

BARTENDER'S NOTES: *This drink is really only as good as the chocolate sauce, so I suggest making your own (page 151) or buying a good-quality brand (one of my favorites is made by King's Cupboard). Though the drink is tasty with standard-issue chocolate sauce, every time I've tasted that version, it has seemed like something was missing. Lacking time to make the cinnamon agave, simply use agave syrup and make sure the glass rim is nicely crusted with the cinnamon sugar.*

To make Cinnamon Sugar, mix 2 parts granulated sugar with 1 part ground cinnamon, preferably Mexican canela.

Cinnamon Sugar (see Bartender's Notes)

1½ ounces 100% blue agave blanco tequila (see page 95)

½ ounce crème de cacao

½ ounce Cinnamon Agave Syrup (page 150)

½ ounce best-quality chocolate sauce, store-bought or homemade (page 151), at room temperature

6 to 10 ice cubes (about ¾ cup)

Spread the Cinnamon Sugar on a small plate. Moisten the rim of a 6-ounce martini glass with a wet paper towel and upend the glass onto the sugar to crust the rim.

In a cocktail shaker, combine the tequila, crème de cacao, Cinnamon Agave Syrup and chocolate sauce. Cover and shake for 10 seconds to blend in the chocolate sauce. Add the ice and shake vigorously until frothy and cold; tiny ice crystals will appear in the drink after about 15 seconds of shaking. Strain into the sugar-crusted glass and serve immediately.

Pitcher Recipe for a Party

MAKES 8 COCKTAILS

1½ cups 100% blue agave blanco tequila (see page 95)

½ cup crème de cacao liqueur

½ cup Cinnamon Agave Syrup (see recipe below)

½ cup best-quality chocolate sauce, store-bought or homemade (page 151), at room temperature

Cinnamon Sugar (see Bartender's Notes)

6 cups ice cubes

In a pitcher, combine the tequila, crème de cacao, Cinnamon Agave Syrup and chocolate sauce and stir until the chocolate sauce is dissolved. Cover and refrigerate until chilled, about 2 hours.

Crust the rims of eight 6-ounce martini glasses with ground Cinnamon Sugar as described in the Bartender's Recipe. Fill a cocktail shaker half full with ice and pour in ¾ cup of the cocktail mixture. Shake and strain into two of the prepared glasses. Repeat for the remaining cocktails.

Cinnamon Agave Syrup

MAKES A GENEROUS ¾ CUP

- ¾ cup agave syrup (light organic syrup gives the best flavor) or Rich Simple Syrup (page 21)

- 5 inches stick cinnamon (preferably Mexican *canela*)

In a small saucepan, combine the agave or simple syrup and 2 tablespoons water. Set over medium heat and add the cinnamon. When the mixture reaches a simmer, simmer for 2 minutes, then remove from the heat and cool to room temperature. Strain.

The syrup will keep a month or more, tightly covered in the refrigerator.

Chocolate Sauce

MAKES 2 CUPS

- 1 cup heavy cream
  ¼ cup Cinnamon Agave Syrup
  (page 150) or corn syrup
- 8 ounces bittersweet chocolate,
  chopped into small pieces

- ¼ teaspoon ground cinnamon
  (preferably Mexican *canela*) (if
  using corn syrup)
- 2 teaspoons pure vanilla extract

In a medium saucepan, combine the heavy cream and Cinnamon Agave Syrup or corn syrup. Set over medium heat. Let come to a simmer, stirring occasionally. Stir in the chocolate and remove from the heat. Stir frequently until all the chocolate has melted. Stir in the cinnamon and vanilla and cool. Stored covered in the refrigerator, the chocolate sauce will last a couple of months.

Coconut-Vanilla *Horchata* Cocktail

Bartender's Recipe

MAKES 1 COCKTAIL

BARTENDER'S NOTES: *While the Coconut* Horchata *isn't hard to make, it requires a few ingredients that probably aren't in your cupboard. If you can't find the rice flour at your grocery store, it is available online and in practically every Mexican grocery.*

To make Powdered Coconut Sugar, mix equal parts powdered sugar and powdered coconut milk—it's like powdered milk, but made from coconut milk. If you can't find it in your local stores, it's readily available online. Or, lacking powdered coconut milk, simply use all powdered sugar.

Powdered Coconut Sugar (see Bartender's Notes)

1 lime wedge

1½ ounces 100% blue agave añejo tequila (see page 96)

½ ounce fresh lime juice

½ ounce triple sec

1 teaspoon agave syrup (light organic syrup gives the best flavor) or Rich Simple Syrup (page 21)

⅛ teaspoon pure vanilla extract (preferably Mexican, which is the most flowery of all the vanillas)

2 ounces Coconut *Horchata* (page 136)

6 to 10 ice cubes (about ¾ cup)

Spread the Powdered Coconut Sugar on a small plate. Moisten the rim of a 6-ounce martini glass with the lime wedge and upend the glass onto the sugar to crust the rim.

In a cocktail shaker, combine the tequila, lime juice, triple sec, agave or simple syrup, vanilla, Coconut *Horchata* and ice. Cover and shake vigorously until frothy and cold; tiny ice crystals will appear in the drink after about 15 seconds of shaking. Strain into the sugar-crusted glass and serve immediately.

Pitcher Recipe for a Party

MAKES 8 COCKTAILS

1½ cups 100% blue agave añejo tequila (see page 96)

½ cup fresh lime juice

½ cup triple sec

3 scant tablespoons agave syrup (light organic syrup gives the best flavor) or Rich Simple Syrup (page 21)

1 teaspoon pure vanilla extract (preferably Mexican, which is the most flowery of all the vanillas)

2 cups Coconut *Horchata* (page 136)

1 lime wedge

Powdered Coconut Sugar (see Bartender's Notes)

6 cups ice cubes

In a pitcher, combine the tequila, lime juice, triple sec, agave or simple syrup, vanilla and Coconut *Horchata*. Cover and refrigerate until chilled, about 2 hours.

Use the lime and sugar to crust the rims of eight 6-ounce martini glasses as described in the Bartender's Recipe. Fill a cocktail shaker half full with ice and pour in a scant 1¼ cups of the cocktail mixture. Shake and strain into two of the prepared glasses. Repeat for the remaining cocktails.

Cocktail Shakers

Because we're living through a cocktail renaissance, there's no longer any need to hunt for cocktail shakers in restaurant supply houses or antique stores. They're everywhere from discount shops to high-end home furnishing boutiques. But they're not all created equal.

First, there are two distinct types of cocktail shakers. The closed cocktail shaker typically consists of a stainless-steel canister (often called a tin), a top with a built-in strainer spout and a little cap to seal the top while shaking. The Boston shaker is only the stainless-steel canister (or tin) plus a similar-looking, slightly smaller glass—usually a pint glass. The first type of shaker is the most common, and it's the easiest to use: measure the drink ingredients into the canister, secure the top and the little cap, shake, remove the cap and strain through the spout into a glass. The Boston shaker requires a bit more experience, though some think the added space it offers for shaking creates a better cocktail. To use it, most bartenders measure the drink ingredients into the glass (some still come with graded ingredient measurements printed on the side), upend the stainless canister on top (tipped *slightly* to one side), give it a rap with the heel of the hand to seat the canister and seal the two parts together, flip the whole thing over—so the stainless canister is on the bottom—and shake. Now, here's the trickiest part: with the heel of the hand, rap the stainless canister near its top—at about the point where it connects to the glass—to break the seal. If the two don't come apart immediately, rap it again or grasp around the top of the stainless canister and squeeze to release the seal. With a Hawthorn (the one with the coiled spring) or julep (perforated bowl-shaped) strainer, strain the drink into your chosen glass.

seven

A Year of Guacamoles

A Master Class
in Guacamoles

That's plural because there are many guacamoles in the Frontera world. We've always offered a really classic guacamole, of course, and it's made with fresh local tomatoes during our season, with sun-drieds the rest of the year. We offer monthly modern guacamoles too (many inspired the recipes that follow). And there are the utterly naked guacamoles made from lightly seasoned mashed avocado, the kind of guacamole that becomes a delicious component when composing plates of empanaditas, flautas or the like.

No matter what flavor guacamole you're making, it's really all about the avocado. And the avocado is one of the most stubborn vegetables (a fruit, really, according to the botanists): It takes a year to mature on the tree, it won't ripen until picked (but, thankfully, it can be cooled and held in an unripe state for a number of months), it's sensitive to temperatures that are too low or high, it bruises easily, and it takes a week or so to ripen from hard to creamy-soft. No ripening contraptions or simple paper bags will hurry that ripening along at any truly useful rate.

Yet an unblemished, buttery-ripe avocado can be a breathtaking wonder. And if yours has been coddled in its cardboard cradle from field to kitchen; if it hasn't been held in its unripe state below about 50 degrees or allowed to get hotter than, say, 75 degrees as it's ripening; and if it hasn't been gassed with a blast of ethylene to rush its softening, it will be a perfect experience. Especially if it's been picked fully mature (oil-rich) from the volcanic soil around Uruapan, Michoacan, the avocado capital of the world. Those are the avocados we use at Frontera, and we manage their journey from field to packing house to ripening room to restaurant kitchen. That's why folks like our guacamole so much: we use great avocados and we ensure that they're treated right.

Turning good avocados into about 3 cups of **Classic Guacamole** is easy, though it requires some restraint. First, prep the vegetables, mixing them together in a bowl: Stem and finely chop **1 large fresh serrano or 1 small fresh jalapeño** (you can split the chile lengthwise and cut out the seeds and veins for a less-spicy guacamole with a more refined texture, but I rarely do). Chop **1 small ripe tomato** into ¼-inch bits (to ensure they won't soften the avocado with too much moisture, we let the tomato drain for a few minutes in a strainer); **OR** finely chop **¼ cup soft sun-dried tomatoes** (the ones that have the texture of a dried apricot). Twist off **a small handful of fresh cilantro** (where the leaves begin) and, holding it tightly bunched, thinly slice across the leaves and tender upper stems. Finely dice **½ small white onion**, scoop into a strainer and run under cold water for 30 seconds or so to "deflame" it; shake off the excess water and measure ⅓ cup.

In a large bowl, coarsely mash the flesh of **3 ripe avocados** (together they should weigh 1 to 1¼ pounds before they're cut): cut each avocado in half around the pit from top to bottom and back up again, twist the halves in opposite directions, pull them apart, remove the pit and scoop the flesh from each half into the bowl). The mashing implement is important: to create thick, "meaty" guacamole, use a large fork or old-fashioned potato or bean masher or the back of a large spoon—we use a large potato masher at Frontera. Gently stir in the vegetables, remembering that you don't have to use them all if it looks like they're going to take focus away from the avocado. Taste what you have, then start the restrained addition of lime: it usually takes **a tablespoon or two of fresh lime juice** to heighten the avocado flavor without screaming "lime juice!" I can assure you that it'll take **about 1 teaspoon**

Preparing Jalapeño Peppers

STEP 1 Cut the jalapeño lengthwise.

STEP 2 Cut out the seeds and veins from each side.

STEP 3 Chop finely.

salt to harmonize the avocado with the other flavors—any less will leave the avocado flavor wandering in the wilderness.

Aside from our Classic Guacamole, the guacamole we rely on the most is flavored with Roasted Tomatillo Salsa. To make about 3 cups **Tomatillo Guacamole**, coarsely mash the flesh of **3 ripe avocados** in a bowl (see the avocados instructions above). Gently stir in 1 cup Roasted Tomatillo Salsa (page 163).

Taste the mixture and season with additional salt, usually a generous ½ teaspoon. It's as simple as that to make this guacamole (we call it "guacamole verde" because of its all-green color), one that's a little more deliciously tangy than what most people are used to—it's got all those tomatillos, after all—and one that is considerably more intriguing, even captivating. It may become your signature guacamole.

Cutting and Pitting Avocados

STEP 1 Cut the avocado in half around the pit from top to bottom and back up again.

STEP 2 Twist the halves in opposite directions

STEP 3 The two avocado halves.

STEP 4 Release the pit from one side with a knife.

STEP 5 Scoop out the flesh from each half.

STEP 6 Coarsely mash the avocado with an old-fashioned potato masher.

Roasted Tomatillo Salsa

MAKES A GENEROUS CUP

- 8 ounces (about 4 medium) tomatillos, husked and rinsed
- 1 large fresh serrano or 1 small jalapeño chile
- 1 large garlic clove, unpeeled
- ½ small white onion, finely chopped
- ¼ cup chopped fresh cilantro
- Salt

Roast the tomatillos on a rimmed baking sheet about 4 inches below a preheated broiler until they're soft and blotchy black on one side, about 5 minutes, then flip them over and roast the other side. Meanwhile, in a small dry skillet, roast the chile and garlic over medium heat, turning them regularly, until soft and dark in spots, about 8 minutes for the chile, 15 minutes for the garlic. Cool everything. Slip the papery skin off the garlic, then combine the tomatillos, chile and garlic in a blender. Process to a coarse puree. Pour into a mixing bowl.

Scoop the chopped onion into a strainer, rinse under cold water and shake off the excess, then measure ⅓ cup. Add the onion to the tomatillo mixture, along with the cilantro. Stir to combine, then taste and season with salt, usually a generous ½ teaspoon. To serve this salsa as a condiment or chip dip, you'll probably want to stir in a little water to loosen the texture. For seasoning guacamole, it's good as is.

F*or many cooks in Mexico,* guacamole is little more than mashed avocado with salt, maybe a squeeze of lime or a hint of garlic or fleck of cilantro. That's really all it needs to be there: Mexican guacamole is a flavor to be daubed onto tacos or tostadas, a creamy condiment to be offered alongside salsas, hot sauces and pickley stuff. It has a singular role, one that rarely includes that of chip dip. Truthfully, the notion of chip dips owes more to our American way of eating than to a Mexican one.

That said, I *love* guacamole and chips, and I love the way avocados are so welcoming to flavors as diverse as fruit and nuts and practically anything from a pig. For years we've been making seasonal guacamoles at Frontera Grill and Topolobampo, inspired mostly by ingredients our local farmers bring to our back door. The recipes that follow here have been gleaned from those offerings—a year of guacamoles for cooks who like to think outside the box.

In the spring, our Midwestern soil sprouts with ramps practically before anything else, and their bold, garlicky flavor is best tamed by slow cooking—something that I think is done best over smoldering embers. Grilled ramps—you can have green onions stand in for them—bring out the savory, herby side of avocado's flavor. (The same goes for grilled garlic chives, which are a personal favorite when ramps are no longer in season.) Add crispy bits of bacon and sweet-tart roasted tomatillos, and you'll have a bowlful of delicious memories. Making guacamole with watercress also highlights avocado's herbal characteristics, but adding sesame will lead you to recognize that there's a lot of nuttiness in avocado's flavor too.

For those of us who cook in Chicago, strawberries follow the spring ramps and watercress, and in a guacamole, they focus the fruity side of an avocado's flavor.

A habanero, though spicy, is packed with tropical fruity flavor that's as explosive as the chile's heat. Combine strawberries, avocado and habanero, embroidered with a little orange and lime, for a guacamole that everyone welcomes in spring.

There are almost too many choices for guacamole add-ins during the summer. Practically any fresh pepper or chile I see at the farmers' market can be roasted and chopped to flavor guacamole. Here I've included a super-chunky version that's all about grill-roasted poblanos plus grilled corn—the kind of guacamole that begs to be served as a condiment for grilled shrimp or chicken.

Summer is all about fruit too, and I've devised one guacamole that features the deep, rich flavor of blackberries and another that showcases juicy watermelon. Before you try to imagine the color of blackberries mashed into avocados, I will assure you that this is a modern guacamole: The base is rather simple, avocado infused with a little mint, roasted red onion and roasted jalapeño; the blackberry comes in the form of little agar-set gels (I call them "jewels") flavored with a little smoky mezcal. This is a "look at me" guacamole.

Watermelon may not seem an intuitive

addition to the richness of mashed avocado, but in the guacamole included here, it provides welcome little bursts of refreshment—especially since the fruit is macerated with a little tequila and the avocado is seasoned with spicy fresh ginger.

As fall settles in, my attention focuses on making the most of our waning tomato season. There are so many varied tomato flavors available at our farmers' markets then—one stall had twenty-eight heirloom varieties last year—that I wanted to develop a guacamole that showed them off in a new way. I've done classic guacamole with tomato, a bacon-and-tomato guacamole and a tomato-basil guacamole with fresh cheese, and I love them all. Pickling a variety of fall vegetables (cauliflower, carrots, onions and jalapeños) and mixing them with ripe-ripe tomatoes and avocados is another delicious, perfectly seasonal winner.

Apples and fennel are iconic fall offerings, and they can be woven together with avocado if you slow-roast the fennel (and chop it fine) and soak the little cubes of apple in lime juice. Fall brings the transition to citrus too, and grapefruit has long been known to be a great combination with avocado. A guacamole that combines avocado with grapefruit and toasty almonds plays with both the fruity and the nutty aspects of avocado's flavor.

The richest guacamoles are my winter ones. Chicharrón, that crackling-crisp pork rind sold in all Mexican groceries, in guacamole, with the addition of tangy Mexican hot sauce and aged *añejo* cheese, is as satisfying a bite as you'll ever have. Same goes for creamy avocados mixed with a mortar-pounded mixture of toasted walnuts and roasted poblano chile, all sprinkled with sweet-tart pomegranate seeds. But the show-stealer here is the Brown-Butter Guacamole with Porcini and Crab. The brown butter blasts the avocado flavor with rich nuttiness, while the bits of rehydrated porcini add depth and complexity. The crab embraces it all—the butter, avocado and mushroom, as well as the tickle of árbol chile and fresh herbs. It's simply spectacular.

Guacamole with Bacon, Grilled Ramps (or Green Onions) and Roasted Tomatillos

MAKES ABOUT 3 CUPS

COOK'S NOTES: Ramps are only available in the spring and only in certain parts of the United States; if yours is the area, you'll probably only find them at farmers' markets or specialty shops. Garlic chives (they look like chives but are flat, with a definite garlic aroma) are typically in abundance in Asian markets; they're perennial and easy to grow, which is what I do. I love them sautéed or grilled for their sweet, green garlicky flavor. Green onions are easy to find everywhere, every day.

IDEAS FOR SERVING: *When I've got my grill going, I like to make my almost-Oaxacan tlayudas: I spread out commercially made tortillas (I buy them from a local tortillería and let them cool off completely) into a single layer, brush both sides of each one lightly but thoroughly with oil, then grill them until they're crisp. Once they cool, I break them into big rustic pieces for dipping into this guacamole. Wedges of grilled pita make a delicious and unexpected vehicle for dipping. For a pass-around appetizer, slices of crispy grilled baguette topped with a dollop of bacony guacamole are always a hit.*

4 medium (about 8 ounces total) tomatillos, husked, rinsed and cut in half crosswise

4 ramps (wild spring leeks) or large green onions
OR a 1-inch-diameter bunch of garlic chives

A little olive or vegetable oil

1 large fresh serrano or small fresh jalapeño, stemmed

4 thick slices (about 4 ounces) bacon

3 ripe medium-large avocados

2 tablespoons fresh lime juice

About 2 tablespoons chopped fresh cilantro, plus extra leaves for garnish

Salt

Heat a gas grill to medium or light a charcoal grill and let it burn until the coals are medium-hot and covered with gray ash. Lay the halved tomatillos cut side down on a rimmed baking sheet or metal baking pan and slide onto the grill. Brush the ramps (or green onions or garlic chives) with oil. Lay them directly on the grill, along with the chile (no oil needed). Grill the ramps (or their stand-ins) and the chile, turning occasionally, until soft and richly browned—the ramps will take 4 to 5 minutes, the chile about 10. Cook the tomatillos about 3 to 4 minutes, until soft and browned on one side, then flip them over and cook the other side. Cool everything. Finely chop the ramps (etc.) and chile, then scrape into a large bowl. Chop the tomatillo into small pieces and scrape them in with the ramps, then scrape in any juice that remains on the baking sheet.

While the grilled vegetables are cooling, cook the bacon in a single layer in a large skillet over medium heat, turning every once in a while, until browned and crispy, about 10 minutes. Drain on paper towels, then chop into small pieces.

Cut the avocados in half, running a knife around the pit from top to bottom and back up again. Twist the halves in opposite directions to release the pit from one side of each avocado. Remove the pit, then scoop the flesh from each half into the bowl with the tomatillos. With an old-fashioned potato masher, a large fork or the back of a large spoon, coarsely mash the avocado with the tomatillo mixture. Stir in the lime juice, cilantro and *half* of the bacon. Taste and season with salt, usually about 1 teaspoon. Cover with plastic wrap pressed directly on the surface of the guacamole and refrigerate until you're ready to serve.

When that time comes, scrape the guacamole into a serving dish and sprinkle with the remaining bacon. Garnish with cilantro leaves.

Guacamole with Bacon, Grilled Ramps (or Green Onions) and Roasted Tomatillos (page 167) >>>

Guacamole with Watercress and Sesame

MAKES ABOUT 3 CUPS

COOK'S NOTES: The earthiness of sesame comes from tahini here, while that distinctive toastiness comes from toasted seeds. If you have a bottle of toasted sesame oil in the cabinet, drizzle in 4 or 5 drops just to add a third sesame dimension.

IDEAS FOR SERVING: *Sesame is delicious with practically any fresh vegetable, so slice up whatever's available for your guests to use for dipping. Tortilla chips are great too: the toasted corn flavor marries beautifully with toasted sesame.*

3 garlic cloves, unpeeled

1 large fresh serrano or 1 small jalapeño, stemmed

1½ tablespoons sesame seeds

3 ripe medium-large avocados

2 tablespoons tahini

½ medium white onion, chopped into pieces no larger than ¼ inch (⅓ cup)

¾ cup (loosely packed) watercress leaves, plus extra for garnish

2 tablespoons fresh lime juice

Salt

In a small dry skillet, roast the garlic and green chile over medium heat, turning regularly, until they're soft and splotchy black in places—about 5 to 10 minutes for the chile, 15 minutes for the garlic. Cool. Peel the papery skin off the garlic, then finely chop the garlic and chile. Scoop into a large bowl.

While the garlic and chile are roasting, measure the sesame seeds into another small skillet and set over medium heat. Stir until they are fragrant and golden, 4 to 5 minutes. Cool.

Cut the avocados in half, running a knife around the pit from top to bottom and back up again. Twist the halves in opposite directions to release the pit from one side of each avocado. Remove the pit, then scoop the flesh from each half into the bowl with the garlic.

Measure the tahini into the bowl, along with *1 tablespoon* of the toasted sesame seeds. With an old-fashioned potato masher, a large fork or the back of a large spoon, coarsely mash the avocado with everything that's in the bowl, mixing it evenly.

Scoop the chopped onion into a strainer, rinse under cold water, shake off the excess and add to the bowl. Gather the watercress leaves together and slice them thinly into a chiffonade. Add them to the bowl, along with the lime juice. Stir gently to combine, then taste and season with salt, usually about 1 teaspoon. Cover with plastic wrap pressed directly on the surface of the guacamole and refrigerate until you're ready to serve the guacamole.

When that time comes, scoop the guacamole into a serving bowl, decorate with watercress and sprinkle with the remaining sesame seeds.

Guacamole with Strawberries and Habanero

MAKES ABOUT 3 CUPS

COOK'S NOTES: The better the strawberries, the better the guacamole. That's why I make this guacamole only during the few weeks when our local strawberries are in season. Habaneros, while very spicy, are jam-packed with flavor; use the quantity that's right for you. You may want to wear gloves while working with the habanero, to avoid painful experiences when inadvertently touching tender parts of your anatomy.

IDEAS FOR SERVING: *Jícama is probably the best "chip" for this very fresh-tasting guacamole, though thin tortilla chips work well too. To tell the truth, a bowl of strawberries is always welcome. Encourage your guests to dip them in. Honest. They'll thank you.*

3 ripe medium-large avocados

½ medium red onion, chopped into pieces no larger than ¼ inch (⅓ cup)

½ to 1 fresh habanero, stemmed, seeded, deveined and finely chopped

1 lime

1 small orange

3 tablespoons loosely packed chopped fresh cilantro

⅔ cup (about 4 ounces) chopped ripe strawberries, plus a little extra for garnish

Salt

Cut the avocados in half, running a knife around the pit from top to bottom and back up again. Twist the halves in opposite directions to release the pit from one side of each avocado. Remove the pit, then scoop the flesh from each half into a large bowl. With an old-fashioned potato masher, a large fork or the back of a large spoon, coarsely mash the avocado.

Scoop the onion into a strainer, rinse under cold water, shake off the excess and then add to the avocado, along with the habanero.

Finely grate the zest (colored part only) from the citrus: you need about 1½ teaspoons grated lime zest and about ½ teaspoon grated orange zest. Add them to the bowl, then juice both fruits and add 2 tablespoons lime juice and 1 tablespoon orange juice to the bowl.

Add the chopped cilantro and strawberries, then carefully stir everything together. Taste and season with salt, usually about 1 teaspoon. Cover with plastic wrap pressed directly on the guacamole and refrigerate until you're ready to serve.

At the last moment, scoop the guacamole into a serving bowl and sprinkle with chopped strawberries.

Grilled Corn and Poblano Guacamole

MAKES ABOUT 4 CUPS

COOK'S NOTES: If you don't have epazote, don't worry. Cilantro is good here, too, though you may want to add an extra tablespoon.

IDEAS FOR SERVING: *Because this is such a substantial guacamole (a fact I emphasize by having you dice part of the avocado), I like to serve it less as a dip for chips and more as an accompaniment to smoky grilled shrimp, chicken, fish or pork. (You've already got the grill hot, so you might as well use it as much as possible.)*

½ medium white onion, sliced crosswise into 3 rounds

A little olive or vegetable oil

Salt

1 small ear of fresh corn, husked and cleaned of silk

1 fresh poblano chile

3 ripe medium-large avocados

¼ cup crumbled Mexican fresh cheese (*queso fresco*) or other fresh cheese, like salted pressed farmer's cheese or goat cheese

2 tablespoons fresh lime juice

1 to 2 tablespoons chopped fresh epazote

Heat a gas grill to medium or light a charcoal fire and let it burn until medium-hot and the coals are covered with gray ash. Lightly brush both sides of the onion slices with oil, sprinkle with salt and lay on the grill. Oil the corn and lay it beside the onion, along with the poblano (no oil needed on it). When the onion slices are browned on one side, 4 to 5 minutes, flip them and grill the other side. Turn the corn regularly until evenly browned, about 5 minutes. Roast the poblano for 5 to 7 minutes, turning it until evenly blackened. Let the roasted vegetables cool.

Chop the onion into ¼-inch pieces. Cut the kernels from the corn (you need about ¾ cup). Rub the blackened skin off the poblano, pull out and discard the stem and seed pod, tear the chile open and briefly rinse to remove stray seeds and bits of blackened skin. Cut into ¼-inch pieces.

Cut the avocados in half, running a knife around the pit from top to bottom and back up again. Twist the halves in opposite directions to release the pit from one side of each avocado. Remove the pit, then scoop the flesh from 1 avocado into a large bowl. Scoop the flesh from the other 2 avocados onto a cutting board and cut into ½-inch pieces. With

an old-fashioned potato masher, a large fork or the back of a large spoon, thoroughly mash the avocado that's in the bowl.

Scoop the diced avocado into the bowl, along with the grilled onion, corn, poblano and *2 tablespoons* of the fresh cheese. Sprinkle with the lime juice and epazote, then gently stir the mixture to distribute everything evenly. Taste and season with salt, usually about 1 teaspoon. Cover with plastic wrap pressed directly on the surface of the guacamole and refrigerate.

When you're ready to serve, scoop the guacamole into a serving bowl and sprinkle with the remaining cheese.

Roasted Jalapeño Guacamole with Blackberry-Mezcal Jewels

MAKES ABOUT 3 CUPS

COOK'S NOTES: Unexpected as it may seem, blackberry and mezcal play beautifully together. And that combo is delicious with an herby, roasty guacamole. Problem is, if you mash the blackberries into the guacamole, the color is, well, less than appealing. That's why I feature the blackberry in the form of an agar-set gel—agar-set because the texture is crisp-tender rather than the typical gelatin bounciness. If you've never used agar before as a gelling agent (available in specialty and natural foods groceries and online), you have nothing to worry about. It's as easy to work with as gelatin. If the loaf pan you have for "casting" the blackberry jewels is a little larger than 8 x 4 inches, it's okay. They'll just be a little thinner.

IDEAS FOR SERVING: *This guacamole is so beautiful that I like to serve it in a wide, flat, light-colored serving dish so that you can see all the Blackberry-Mezcal Jewels. It makes a beautiful pass-around appetizer too, little spoonfuls of guacamole on beet and sweet potato chips, each garnished with a few of the dark purple jewels and a small mint leaf.*

½ medium red onion, sliced crosswise into 3 rounds

1 large fresh jalapeño, stemmed

3 ripe medium-large avocados

2 tablespoons chopped fresh mint leaves, plus small whole leaves for garnish

½ teaspoon black pepper, preferably freshly ground

2 tablespoons fresh lime juice

Salt

A scant cup Blackberry-Mezcal Jewels (page 179)

Heat a large skillet over medium. Lay the onion rounds in a single layer on a small piece of foil and slide onto the hot skillet. Lay the jalapeño in the pan. Roast until the onion is soft and brown, about 5 minutes per side, and the jalapeño is soft and blotchy black in places—you'll have to turn it regularly for about 10 minutes. Cool.

Finely chop the onion and jalapeño and scoop into a large bowl.

Cut the avocados in half, running a knife around the pit from top to bottom and back up again. Twist the halves in opposite directions to release the pit from one side of each

avocado. Remove the pit, then scoop the flesh from each half into the bowl with the jalapeño mixture. With an old-fashioned potato masher, a large fork or the back of a large spoon, coarsely mash the avocado with the jalapeño mixture.

Stir in the chopped mint, black pepper and lime juice, then taste and season with salt, usually about 1 teaspoon. Cover with plastic wrap pressed directly on the surface of the guacamole and refrigerate until you're ready to serve.

At the last moment, scoop the guacamole into a wide shallow serving dish and sprinkle with the Blackberry-Mezcal Jewels and small mint leaves.

Blackberry-Mezcal Jewels

MAKES ABOUT 2½ CUPS

- 4 ounces (about ¾ cup) blackberries
- 1 tablespoon sugar
- 1 teaspoon salt

- 4 teaspoons (3 grams) agar flakes (see Cook's Notes)
- ⅓ cup mezcal (you can use tequila, but you'll miss the beautiful smokiness)

In a blender, combine the blackberries, ⅓ cup water, the sugar and salt. Blend to a smooth puree. Strain into a small saucepan to remove the seeds.

Whisk in the agar, set over medium heat and bring to a simmer. Cook, stirring regularly, for 5 minutes to dissolve the agar. Remove from the heat, stir in the mezcal and immediately pour into an 8 x 4-inch loaf pan. Let cool to room temperature (the mixture will thicken and begin to firm), then refrigerate until fully set.

When ready to use, run a knife around the edges of the blackberry gel to loosen it. Flip the loaf pan upside down onto a cutting board and press on the center of the loaf pan to release the gel. Cut the gel into cubes that are as wide as your gel is thick.

Watermelon-Ginger Guacamole

MAKES ABOUT 3 CUPS

COOK'S NOTES: I've called for compressing the watermelon using a vacuum sealer like a FoodSaver in order to compact its texture and flavor; "compressed watermelon" is the most beautiful and intensely flavored watermelon in the world. Sprinkling it with a little tequila before vacuum-sealing forces the boozy flavor into the watermelon, taking the watermelon from Wow! delicious to No Way! delicious. (I cleaned that up a little bit for publication.) Bottom line: vacuum-sealing the watermelon is very tasty and cool, but not a deal breaker. You can simply sprinkle the watermelon cubes with tequila, let them stand for a few minutes and continue with the recipe.

IDEAS FOR SERVING: *Though this is a chip dip that will get your guests really excited, it's also really delicious scooped onto slices of jicama or seedless cucumber and served as a pass-around appetizer.*

1 cup (6 ounces) cubed seedless watermelon (¼-inch dice)—you'll need about a 1-pound chunk of watermelon

2 tablespoons blanco tequila

3 ripe medium-large avocados

1 lime

A small piece of fresh ginger

1 fresh red jalapeño or Fresno chile, stemmed, seeded if you wish and finely chopped

1 to 2 tablespoons chopped fresh herb, like mint or cilantro

Salt

Scoop the watermelon cubes into a vacuum-sealing bag, sprinkle in the tequila and then vacuum-seal. Refrigerate while you're making the guacamole.

Cut the avocados in half, running a knife around the pit from top to bottom and back up again. Twist the halves in opposite directions to release the pit from one side of each avocado. Remove the pit, then scoop the flesh from each half into a large bowl. With an old-fashioned potato masher, a large fork or the back of a large spoon, coarsely mash the avocado.

Grate the zest from half of the lime into the avocado. Juice the lime and squeeze in 2 tablespoons juice.

Finely grate the ginger. Measure about ½ teaspoon and add it to the avocado, along with the chile and herb. Stir to combine, then taste and season with salt, usually about 1 teaspoon. Cover with plastic wrap pressed directly on the surface of the guacamole and refrigerate until serving time.

Right before carrying the guacamole to your guests, release the vacuum-seal on the watermelon. Gently stir *half* of it into the guacamole, scoop the mixture into a serving dish and top with the remaining watermelon.

Heirloom Tomato and Pickled Vegetable Guacamole

MAKES ABOUT 3 CUPS

COOK'S NOTES: Many of the brands of store-bought pickled jalapeño mixtures are skimpy on the vegetables. That's why I've included a very simple recipe for making pickled jalapeños with the proportions I like—much more along the lines of the home-made mixtures you can buy in many markets in Mexico.

IDEAS FOR SERVING: *For me, this is a total chip-and-dip guacamole. So buy really good tortilla chips, or make them, and, if you're game, put out broken pieces of fresh, crispy chicharrón for an amazing (and very authentic) dipping experience. For a pass-around appetizer, cut the pickled jalapeños in half, scoop out the seeds and fill them with the guacamole. If jalapeños seem too much, the same can be done with tiny romaine, Little Gem lettuce or endive leaves.*

1 medium heirloom tomato, chopped into ¼ inch pieces (you need 1 cup), plus a little extra for garnish

1 large pickled jalapeño, store-bought or home-made (page 185) stemmed, seeded if you wish and finely chopped

About ½ cup chopped (¼-inch pieces) pickled vegetables—onions, carrots, cauliflower—from the pickled jalapeños, plus a little extra for garnish

3 ripe medium-large avocados

¼ cup loosely packed roughly chopped fresh cilantro, plus a little for garnish if you like

Salt

A little pickling liquid from the jalapeños, if needed

Scoop the tomato into a strainer, set it over a bowl and let drain for a few minutes, while you're preparing the other ingredients.

In a large bowl, combine the chopped jalapeño and pickled vegetables. Cut the avocados in half, running a knife around the pit from top to bottom and back up again. Twist the halves in opposite directions to release the pit from one side of each avocado. Remove the pit, then scoop the flesh from each half into the bowl. With an old-fashioned potato masher, a large fork or the back of a large spoon, coarsely mash the avocado with the chile and pickled vegetables.

Mix in the cilantro, taste and season with salt, usually about 1 teaspoon. Taste again;

if the guacamole seems to need a little more tang, add some of the jalapeño pickling liquid. Cover with plastic wrap pressed directly on the surface of the guacamole and refrigerate until serving time. When you're ready, scoop the guacamole into a serving bowl and sprinkle with chopped tomato, pickled vegetables and cilantro, if you wish.

Quick Pickled Jalapeños with cauliflower, carrots and herbs

MAKES ABOUT 4 CUPS

- 5 (about 5 ounces) large jalapeños
- 1 cup apple cider vinegar
- 1 teaspoon salt
- ½ teaspoon cracked black pepper
- A generous teaspoon of mixed dried *hierbas de olor*—thyme, marjoram, Mexican oregano

- 2 medium (about 4 ounces total) carrots, peeled and sliced crosswise no thicker than ¼ inch
- ¼ small head cauliflower, broken or cut into small pieces no larger than ½ inch (1 generous cup)
- ½ medium white onion, sliced ¼ inch thick

Cut a 2-inch slit down the side of each jalapeño. In a large saucepan, measure the vinegar, 1 cup water, the salt, pepper and herbs. Bring to a boil, add the jalapeños, reduce the heat to medium and simmer for 3 minutes.

Combine the carrot, cauliflower and onion in a heatproof storage container large enough to hold the jalapeños too. After the jalapeños have simmered 3 minutes, transfer them and their pickling juice to the storage container. Cool, then refrigerate overnight, or until you're ready to use them.

Apple-Fennel Guacamole

MAKES ABOUT 3 CUPS

IDEAS FOR SERVING: *This is a guacamole to put on a dressed-up table with lots of fresh vegetables for dipping, maybe some garlic toasts or grilled pita, even some rustic tortilla chips. That said, my favorite way to serve it is as a condiment with grilled chicken or fish on an Indian-summer afternoon sitting in my backyard. Which happens far too infrequently.*

1 medium fennel bulb, stalks and fronds cut off

1 tablespoon olive oil

Salt

½ medium apple (a crisp-textured one like Granny Smith works well here), peeled, cored and cut into ¼-inch pieces

2 tablespoons fresh lime juice

3 ripe medium-large avocados

1 generous teaspoon chopped fresh thyme

1 large fresh serrano or 1 small jalapeño, stemmed, seeded if you wish and finely chopped

Heat the oven to 350 degrees. Cut the fennel bulb in half, then cut each half into 3 wedges. Lay them in a single layer in a small baking dish and drizzle with the olive oil. Measure in ¼ cup water, sprinkle with ½ teaspoon salt, cover with foil and slide into the oven. Bake until the fennel is tender, about 1 hour. Cool.

Remove the fennel to a cutting board and pull off any exterior layers that seem fibrous. Cut out and discard the pieces of core that hold each wedge together, then chop the remainder into tiny pieces—the tinier the better.

While the fennel is cooking, scoop the apple into a bowl, sprinkle it with the lime juice and toss to combine. Refrigerate until you're ready to use it.

Cut the avocados in half, running a knife around the pit from top to bottom and back up again. Twist the halves in opposite directions to release the pit from one side of each avocado. Remove the pit, then scoop the flesh from each half into a large bowl. With an old-fashioned potato masher, a large fork or the back of a large spoon, coarsely mash the avocado.

Add the thyme, chopped green chile, apples (including all the lime juice) and *half* of the chopped fennel to the avocado and stir to combine. (Refrigerate the remaining fennel to add to a salad or pasta dish.) Taste and season with salt, usually about 1 teaspoon. Cover with plastic wrap pressed directly on the surface of the guacamole and refrigerate until serving time.

When you're ready for the guacamole, scoop it into a serving dish and carry it to your guests.

Almond-Grapefruit Guacamole

MAKES ABOUT 3 CUPS

COOK'S NOTE: I've made this guacamole with and without the almond butter, and while it's really tasty without, the almond butter infuses every bite with a rich nuttiness that I love.

IDEAS FOR SERVING: *This is an impressive chip-dip guacamole for winter, when both avocados and grapefruit are at their peak. Its citrusy lightness goes well with raw vegetable "chips"—think jícama, sunchoke, small Japanese white turnip. But don't overlook this guacamole as part of a light entrée or first course: spoon the guacamole into leaves of endive, romaine hearts or Little Gem lettuce and top with shrimp (grilled—or seared on a grill pan—and cooled).*

1 ounce (about ⅓ cup) sliced almonds

1 small grapefruit (preferably pink)

3 ripe medium-large avocados

2 tablespoons almond butter (see Cook's Note)

½ medium white onion, chopped into pieces no larger than ¼ inch (⅓ cup)

1 fresh serrano or small jalapeño, stemmed, seeded if you wish and finely chopped

2 tablespoons chopped fresh herb—like cilantro, parsley, basil, mint or even lemon balm or lemon verbena, if you can lay your hands on it

Salt

Heat the oven to 325 degrees. Spread the sliced almonds onto a baking sheet, slide into the oven and bake until lightly golden and aromatic, about 10 minutes. Cool.

Stand the grapefruit on a cutting board, stem end up. With a sharp knife, cut off the rind (colored zest and white pith) and top layer of membrane, exposing the grapefruit flesh. (I find it easiest to cut from top to bottom, following the curve of the fruit.) The membrane that separates the segments will be clearly visible as thin white lines running from the grapefruit's top to bottom. Working over a bowl, holding the grapefruit in one hand, cut toward the center along either side of each membrane, releasing membraneless segments (aka suprêmes). When all the segments have been removed, squeeze the juice from what remains of the grapefruit into the bowl. You need about 3 tablespoons to season the guacamole. Chop or break the grapefruit suprêmes into ½-inch pieces. Measure ¾ cup.

Cut the avocados in half, running a knife around the pit from top to bottom and back up again. Twist the halves in opposite directions to release the pit from one side of each

avocado. Remove the pit, then scoop the flesh from each half into a large bowl. Measure in the almond butter. With an old-fashioned potato masher, a large fork or the back of a large spoon, coarsely mash the avocado and almond butter together.

Scoop the chopped onion into a strainer, rinse it under cold water, shake off the excess and add it to the avocado. Add the ¾ cup grapefruit segments, the 3 tablespoons grape-fruit juice, the chopped chile and fresh herb and *half* of the toasted sliced almonds. Stir to combine, taste and season with salt, usually about 1 teaspoon. Cover with plastic wrap pressed directly on the surface of the gua-camole and refrigerate until you're ready to serve (best within a couple of hours).

When you're ready for the guacamole, scoop it into a serving dish and sprinkle with the remaining toasted almonds.

Roasted Tomatillo Guacamole with Crunchy Chicharrón

MAKES ABOUT 3 CUPS

COOK'S NOTES: Everything for this guacamole is available at a good grocery store—except, perhaps, the chicharrón, Mexican hot sauce and *queso añejo*. Visiting a Mexican market will certainly provide what you're after, though you have other options: crispy pork rinds can stand in for the similar chicharrón, your favorite hot sauce can stand in for the Mexican variety, and Pecorino Romano cheese can be substituted for the *queso añejo*.

IDEAS FOR SERVING: *Because getting chicharrón, hot sauce and* queso añejo *in every bite is my favorite part of this guacamole, I like to serve it in the avocado skin or a wide shallow bowl topped with an even layer of the chicharrón, drizzled with hot sauce and sprinkled with the grated cheese. Passing a tray of sturdy tortilla chips or little tostadas (baked or fried) topped with fully garnished dollops of the guacamole ensures that everyone gets a perfect bite. While tortilla chips are the perfect scoop here, I've been known to put out baskets of chicharrón for scooping too.*

4 medium (about 8 ounces total) tomatillos, husked and rinsed

3 ripe medium-large avocados

½ medium white onion, chopped into pieces no larger than ¼ inch (about ⅓ cup)

2 tablespoons fresh lime juice

2 tablespoons chopped fresh cilantro

Salt

A 1-ounce piece of crispy chicharrón (preferably a freshly made one from a Mexican grocery store)

A couple of tablespoons of Mexican hot sauce like Tamazula, Valentina or Búfalo

About ¼ cup grated Mexican aged cheese (*queso añejo*) or other garnishing cheese, like Pecorino Romano or Parmesan

Roast the tomatillos on a rimmed baking sheet about 4 inches below a preheated broiler until soft and blotchy black on one side, about 6 minutes. Flip and roast the other side. Cool.

Scoop the tomatillos onto a cutting board, leaving most of their juice behind. (They'll have softened to the point of almost falling apart.) Chop them into rough ¼-inch pieces and scrape them into a large bowl.

Roasted Tomatillo Guacamole with Crunchy Chicharrón >>>

Cut the avocados in half, running a knife around the pit from top to bottom and back up again. Twist the halves in opposite directions to release the pit from one side of each avocado. Remove the pit, then scoop the flesh from each half into the bowl with the tomatillos. With an old-fashioned potato masher, a large fork or the back of a large spoon, coarsely mash the avocado and tomatillo together.

Scoop the chopped onion into a strainer, rinse under cold running water, shake off the excess and add to the bowl, along with the lime juice and cilantro. Stir everything to combine, then taste and season with salt, usually about 1 teaspoon. Cover with plastic wrap pressed directly on the surface of the guacamole and refrigerate until ready to serve.

To serve, chop the chicharrón into ¼-inch pieces (as a variation I sometimes "shave" the chicharrón into shards by thinly slicing it) and sprinkle it over the guacamole. Drizzle with the hot sauce and sprinkle with the cheese.

Guacamole with Toasted Walnuts and Pomegranate

MAKES ABOUT 3 CUPS

COOK'S NOTES: If you don't have a Mexican *molcajete* (or other mortar and pestle—a piece of equipment I consider to be one of the most useful), you can pulse the walnuts in a food processor until finely chopped, then add the poblanos and continue to pulse until they are chopped quite fine.

During the summer, before pomegranates are in season, I've done this guacamole sprinkled with diced flame-roasted piquillo, pimento or other farmers' market fresh red peppers.

IDEAS FOR SERVING: *I like to serve this guacamole in a wide flat serving bowl, garnished with the pomegranate seeds and walnuts. I've also been known to sprinkle some crumbled Mexican fresh cheese (*queso fresco*), goat cheese, mild feta or blue cheese on top.*

1 fresh poblano chile

¾ cup walnuts

3 ripe medium-large avocados

½ medium white onion, chopped into pieces no larger than ¼ inch (⅓ cup)

2 tablespoons chopped fresh flat-leaf parsley leaves

2 tablespoons fresh lime juice

Salt

Seeds from ½ medium pomegranate, removed from pith (you need a generous ½ cup)

Roast the poblano over an open flame or 4 inches below a broiler, turning regularly, until blackened all over, about 5 minutes for an open flame, 10 minutes for the broiler. Place in a bowl, cover with a kitchen towel and let cool until handleable. Rub the blackened skin off the chile and pull out the stem and seed pod. Rinse to remove any bits of skin and seed. Roughly chop and scoop into a mortar.

While the chile is cooling, heat the oven to 325 degrees. Spread the walnuts on a baking sheet and bake them until toasty-aromatic, 8 to 10 minutes. Cool.

Scrape about *two-thirds* of the walnuts in with the poblanos; set the remainder aside for garnish. Use the pestle to crush the walnuts and poblanos together to a coarse puree. Scrape the mixture into a large bowl.

Cut the avocados in half, running a knife around the pit from top to bottom and back

up again. Twist the halves in opposite directions to release the pit from one side of each avocado. Remove the pit, then scoop the flesh from each half into the bowl. With an old-fashioned potato masher, a large fork or the back of a large spoon, coarsely mash the avocado with the poblano-walnut mixture.

Scoop the onion into a strainer, rinse under cold water, shake off the excess and add to the avocado, along with the parsley and lime juice. Stir to combine, then taste and season with salt, usually about 1 teaspoon. Cover with plastic wrap pressed directly on the surface of the guacamole and refrigerate until you're ready to serve.

When that moment arrives, scrape the guacamole into a serving dish and sprinkle with the pomegranate seeds and remaining walnuts.

Brown Butter Guacamole with Porcini and Crab

MAKES ABOUT 3 CUPS

COOK'S NOTES: I love jumbo lump crabmeat or plump morsels extracted from Alaskan king crab legs, but those are not always within reach. Use what you like, what's available or what you can afford. Dried porcini, while very special, are available in most well-stocked grocery stores and won't break the bank.

IDEAS FOR SERVING: *This is such a surprising, over-the-top guacamole that I'd serve it in the most beautiful bowl I have, along with unexpected accompaniments for dipping or onto which your guests may want to spread this treat: a variety of root vegetable chips (sweet potato, beet, taro), jícama, crispy toasts or croutons or out-of-the-ordinary crackers. Or make your own tortilla chips and top each one with a spoonful of the guacamole, a bit of crab and an herb leaf. Pass them to your guests—who will never forget these perfect bites.*

¼ ounce (¼ cup) dried porcini mushrooms

2 tablespoons unsalted butter

1 to 2 árbol chiles, stemmed and chopped into
   small pieces

2 garlic cloves, peeled and finely chopped

3 ripe medium-large avocados

1 large green onion, sliced crosswise into
   ⅛-inch-wide pieces

1½ tablespoons fresh lime juice

1 tablespoon chopped fresh sage or parsley,
   plus a little extra for garnish

Salt

4 ounces (about ¾ cup) crabmeat, picked over
   for stray bits of shell, then coarsely shredded

Place the dried porcini in a small bowl, pour on ¼ cup very hot tap water and let soak for 30 minutes.

In a small skillet, melt the butter over medium heat. As the foaming begins to subside, pay close attention: when the butter has turned nut brown and the foaming has subsided, remove the skillet from the heat, add the chopped árbol chile and garlic and stir for a minute, until richly aromatic, then return the pan to the heat. Tip in the porcini soaking liquid and simmer briskly until the mixture begins to sputter (indicating that most of the liquid has evaporated), about 5 minutes. Cool.

Brown Butter Guacamole with Porcini and Crab >>>

Cut the avocados in half, running a knife around the pit from top to bottom and back up again. Twist the halves in opposite directions to release the pit from one side of each avocado. Remove the pit, then scoop the flesh from each half into a large bowl. Add the brown butter mixture (it may have congealed some but it should still be soft). With an old-fashioned potato masher, a large fork or the back of a large spoon, coarsely mash the avocado and butter together.

Chop the drained porcini into little bits and add them to the avocado, along with the sliced green onion, lime juice and sage or parsley. Taste and season with salt, usually about 1 teaspoon. Cover with plastic wrap pressed directly on the surface of the guacamole and refrigerate until you're ready to serve.

When that moment arrives, scoop the guacamole into a serving bowl, scatter the crab over the top and sprinkle with chopped sage or parsley.

{ eight }

Vegetable and Nut Snacks

L ike you, *I've been to too many* parties where the food consisted of a vegetable-and-dip platter from the grocery store. Now, I'm a huge proponent of serving fresh vegetables—they make wonderfully welcome light snacks with drinks—but we have to think beyond that platter, to brighter, bolder, more attractive flavors. If cleaning and slicing or dicing is your concern, lots of produce departments offer a selection of prepared vegetables and fruits (especially if they have a salad bar). And just a few minutes of finishing can turn your choices into such enticing offerings that folks will want to eat because they're truly delicious, not because they think they're the "healthy" option.

Street vendors all over Mexico season cubes, sticks and slices of all kinds of vegetables and fruits (think jícama, cucumber, mango, watermelon, cantaloupe, pineapple) with a sprinkling of lime juice, pure powdered chile and salt. That's the easiest preparation choice you can make, and it's one of my favorites. (If you want to go all out, make your own powdered guajillo or ancho chile [see Cook's Notes, page 207] and mix it with some salt.)

Or go another direction, as I've done in the recipes here: Mix sweet honeydew and cantaloupe with the floral spice of habanero and a little orange. Or pair crunchy jícama with juicy watermelon and dress it with savory sesame and a little red chile. Or season crunchy wedges of raw chayote with jalapeño, mild vinegar and cilantro. Or marinate squares of napa cabbage with lime, spicy árbol chile and fresh herbs. Each one of these preparations can be tossed together in no time and will spark the palate of anyone who tries them. Crunchy, bright, savory, sweet, addictive. Set out toothpicks or cocktail forks and let your guests dig in.

I find a bowl of toasty nuts or seeds to be about the most satisfying pre-dinner nosh imaginable. They never fail to take the edge off my hunger, and, if they're a little spicy and salty, they wake up my taste buds. A little bowl of toasty saltiness is fine, but one that's redolent of chiles, spices and herbs is even more appealing.

That's why I've developed a recipe for pumpkin seeds that you toast in a skillet, then glaze with roasted garlic, green chile and tequila. I also like to bake cashews with a glaze of chipotle, honey and spices, in no small part because they fill the kitchen with the most mouthwatering aroma. And savory sesame, sparked with a little roasted green chile and varnished on toasty pecans, is unexpectedly tasty. The crunch of corn nuts has always been appealing to me, but I'd never investigated how they were made. Turns out they're simple (though you have to plan way ahead): a long soak for an old-fashioned type of dried corn, then an uncomplicated toast in hot oil. For the overachiever: you'll find the details here for making your own fresh-and-toasty corn nuts.

Lime-Pickled Melon

MAKES ABOUT 4 CUPS

COOK'S NOTES: If you have a vacuum sealer (FoodSaver is a common brand), vacuum-seal the honeydew and cantaloupe and wait a couple of minutes, then release the vacuum, add the flavorings (habanero, lime zest and juice, salt) to the bag, re-vacuum and refrigerate. "Compressing" the melons first compacts their texture and concentrates their flavor. After adding the flavors, you won't get as strong a vacuum with a home-model vacuum sealer, but you will get more even penetration of the flavors.

About 1 pound cleaned honeydew melon, cut into 2-inch sticks (*batons* in kitchen-speak) about ½ inch thick (3 cups loosely packed)

About 1 pound cleaned cantaloupe, cut into 2-inch sticks about ½ inch thick (3 cups loosely packed)

1 fresh habanero chile, stemmed, seeded and finely chopped

The finely grated zest from ½ lime

½ cup fresh lime juice

1 teaspoon salt

A couple of tablespoons chopped green onion tops for garnish

In a large bowl, combine the honeydew, cantaloupe and habanero. Add the zest (colored part only), lime juice and salt. Stir to coat the fruit well. Cover and refrigerate for at least 1 hour, stirring regularly to make sure the fruit is being evenly infused with the lime. (This mixture is best served within a few hours of the time it's made.)

Scoop the mixture into a serving bowl, sprinkle with the chopped green onion tops and serve.

Compressing fruit with a FoodSaver

Citrusy Jícama and Watermelon with Toasted Sesame

MAKES ABOUT 4 CUPS

COOK'S NOTES: Pure powdered guajillo chile: I'm calling it "powdered chile," rather than "chile powder" because in the United States the latter means powdered chiles with spices, garlic, sugar and salt added—not what I'm looking for here. You can find pure powdered chile in Mexican groceries and online. If you like it spicy, add a little powdered chipotle/morita chile. Ancho works fine too, though its flavor is deeper and richer—not necessarily better here. If you can't find powdered guajillo chile, you can toast guajillos (torn open, seeded and laid flat on a baking sheet) in a 325-degree oven until they're nearly crisp, about 5 minutes, let them cool, and then powder them in an electric spice grinder or high-speed blender. Four medium guajillos will give you about 3 generous tablespoons of powder.

For the absolute best texture and deepest penetration of flavor, use a vacuum-sealer (FoodSaver is a common brand): Vacuum-seal the jícama and watermelon and wait a couple of minutes. Release the vacuum, add the flavorings (citrus juices, chile, salt, sesame oil) to the bag, re-vacuum and refrigerate for an hour or so.

1½ tablespoons sesame seeds

½ medium jícama, peeled and cut into 1-inch cubes (about 2 cups)

A 3-pound chunk of seedless watermelon, rind cut off and flesh cut into 1-inch cubes (about 3 cups)

¼ cup fresh lime juice

¼ cup fresh orange juice

1 to 2 tablespoons powdered guajillo chile (see Cook's Notes)

1 teaspoon toasted sesame oil (optional but recommended)

Salt

In a small dry skillet, toast the sesame seeds over medium heat, stirring frequently, until golden and aromatic, 2 to 3 minutes. Remove from the heat.

In a large bowl, stir together the jícama, watermelon, citrus juices, *1 tablespoon* of the powdered chile and the sesame oil, if using. Taste and season with salt, usually about 1 teaspoon. If you like, stir in more powdered chile for a bolder-tasting dish. Cover and refrigerate for an hour or so, for the flavors to mingle. (This is best served within a few hours of the time it is made.)

Scoop the mixture into a serving bowl, sprinkle with the toasted sesame seeds and carry to your guests.

Green Chile "Pickled" Chayote

MAKES ABOUT 4 CUPS

COOK'S NOTE: Rice vinegar is milder than most of the vinegars in our American kitchens. It's easily found in well-stocked grocery stores. Champagne or cava vinegar is a good substitute, as are any of the homemade vinegars available in most markets in Mexico.

2 large (about 1¼ pounds total) chayotes, peeled, cored and cut into ¼-inch-thick wedges

2 to 3 fresh jalapeños, stemmed, seeded and thinly sliced lengthwise

1 lime

1 cup rice vinegar (see Cook's Note)

¼ cup sugar

1 teaspoon salt

A handful of fresh cilantro leaves for garnish

In a large bowl, combine the chayote and jalapeños. Grate the zest (colored part only) of the lime on top. Add the vinegar, sugar and salt and stir to coat the chayote well. Cover and let stand at room temperature for at least an hour, stirring regularly to make sure that the vinegar mixture is evenly penetrating the chayote. (The chayote is great 4 or 5 hours after it's made; even refrigerating the chayote, covered, for several days before serving will still offer you a wonderfully crunchy nibble.)

When you're ready to serve, transfer the chayote mixture to a serving bowl and sprinkle with the cilantro leaves.

Limey Red Chile Napa Cabbage

MAKES ABOUT 4 CUPS

COOK'S NOTES: Any of several garnishes will make this snack even more distinctive. You can certainly sprinkle some chopped cilantro or parsley on this little vegetable snack, but don't overlook the more unusual Mexican herbs like epazote or *hoja santa* if they are within your reach. You can buy *charales* (tiny dried minnow-like fish) in Mexican (and a lot of Asian) markets. I like to toast them in a dry pan, then crumble them over the napa just before serving. If you're a real lover of dried fish flavors, stir in a sprinkling of dried shrimp powder.

8 dried árbol (or other small) chiles

1 small head (about 1½ pounds) napa cabbage, cut in half, cored and sliced into pieces about 1 x 2 inches

1 cup fresh lime juice

2 tablespoons sugar

1 teaspoon salt

One or more of the garnishes described in the Cook's Notes.

In a small dry skillet, toast the chiles over medium heat, stirring them nearly continually until they change color slightly and release a toasty aroma, 3 to 4 minutes. Cool, then chop into small pieces. The seeds will naturally fall out as you chop the chiles; collect the chile pieces and discard the seeds.

In a large bowl, combine the cabbage, toasted chile, lime juice, ½ cup water, sugar and salt. Cover and let stand for several hours at room temperature. (I like the napa best after 4 or 5 hours; it changes texture over a couple of days in the refrigerator, but it's still very good.)

Scoop the mixture into a serving bowl, add one or more of the garnishes and serve.

Green Chile Pumpkin Seeds with Tequila and Lime

MAKES 3 CUPS

COOK'S NOTE: I've given you a large recipe for these tasty pumpkin seeds because I like to keep extras in the freezer to have on hand for that perfect little snack before a nice weekend dinner.

3 fresh serrano chiles, stemmed

3 garlic cloves, unpeeled

1 lime

2 tablespoons olive oil

2 tablespoons tequila

1 tablespoon sugar

2 tablespoons chopped fresh cilantro

1 teaspoon salt

3 cups (about 1 pound) hulled raw pumpkin seeds

In a small dry skillet, roast the chiles and garlic over medium heat, turning, until they are soft and blotchy-black in places—about 8 minutes for the chiles, 10 to 15 minutes for the garlic. Cool, then slip off the garlic's papery skin.

In a mortar or small food processor, combine the chiles and garlic. Grate the zest (colored part only) of the lime over the chiles, juice the lime and pour 2 tablespoons of the juice over the chiles. Add the olive oil, tequila, sugar, cilantro and salt. Pound with the mortar or process to as smooth a puree as possible.

Turn on the oven to 350 degrees. In a very large (12-inch) skillet, toast the pumpkin seeds over medium heat, stirring nearly constantly as soon as you hear one pop. When most have popped from flat to oval, about 5 minutes, add the puree and stir to evenly coat, then spread on a rimmed baking sheet lined with parchment or a nonstick baking mat.

Bake until the flavorings have formed a shiny, dryish coating on the seeds, about 15 minutes. Cool, and they're ready to serve. The pumpkin seeds can be stored in an airtight container for a week or so at room temperature or for several months in the freezer.

Sesame–Green Chile Pecans

MAKES 3 CUPS

1 to 2 fresh serrano chiles, stemmed

2 tablespoons sesame seeds

1 egg white

1 tablespoon agave syrup or honey

2 teaspoons Worcestershire sauce

1 teaspoon salt

3 cups (about 10 ounces) raw pecan halves

Turn on the oven to 350 degrees. In a small dry skillet, roast the chile over medium heat, turning frequently, until soft and blackened in spots, about 10 minutes. Remove the chile and add the sesame seeds. Stir regularly until golden and aromatic, about 3 minutes. Set the seeds aside.

Roughly chop the chile and scoop into a small food processor or blender. Add the egg white, agave syrup or honey, Worcestershire and salt. Blend until smooth.

In a large bowl, combine the pecans and green chile mixture. Stir to coat the nuts with the mixture—it'll take longer than you think to get the coating thorough and even. Use your hands or a slotted spoon to scoop the pecans onto a baking sheet lined with parchment or a nonstick baking mat, spreading them into a single uncrowded layer; leave behind the chile mixture that doesn't cling. Then, with a small spoon, drizzle a little of the left-behind mixture directly onto the pecans and sprinkle them with the toasted sesame.

Bake until the nuts are shiny and dryish looking, about 20 minutes. Cool, and they are ready to serve. The nuts can be stored in an airtight container for a week or so at room temperature or for several months in the freezer.

<<< from top: Smoky Spiced Cashews (page 216), Green Chile Pumpkin Seeds with Tequila and Lime (page 213), Sesame–Green Chile Pecans (page 215)

Frontera | **Vegetable and Nut Snacks** **215**

Smoky Spiced Cashews

MAKES 3 CUPS

COOK'S NOTE: If you can't find powdered chipotle, you can use powdered ancho or guajillo (see Cook's Notes, page 207), though the flavor will be a little different.

3 cups (about 1 pound) raw cashews

2 tablespoons olive oil

2 tablespoons agave syrup (light organic gives the best flavor) or honey

1 to 2 teaspoons powdered chipotle chile (see Cook's Note)

½ teaspoon ground black pepper, preferably freshly ground

½ teaspoon ground allspice, preferably freshly ground

1 teaspoon salt

Heat the oven to 350 degrees. In a large bowl, combine all the ingredients, mixing to distribute the spices evenly. Spread the cashews in an uncrowded layer on a rimmed baking sheet lined with parchment or a nonstick baking mat.

Bake, stirring thoroughly every 5 minutes to coat the nuts with the flavorings, until they have a shiny, dryish coating, about 15 minutes. Stir every few minutes as they cool to ensure they don't stick together, and they're ready to serve. The nuts can be stored in an airtight container for several days at room temperature or for several months in the freezer.

Homemade Corn Nuts

MAKES 2 CUPS

COOK'S NOTES: Corn nuts were developed as a way to showcase the tender, floury texture of a large-kernel corn that's popular in Peru. To make them, you need to get the right corn or they won't be tender enough. (I've had best luck using Goya Giant White Corn (Maíz Mole Pelado—available at many well-stocked grocery stores and most Hispanic markets.) Having tried the corn that has been soaked for 1, 2 and 3 days, I can say that it takes the full 3 days to rehydrate the corn enough to turn out tender corn nuts.

You have two choices for toasting the corn: in ¾ inch of oil on the stovetop (this produces the most classic corn-nut texture and flavor, not to mention the greatest tenderness) or with a light coating of oil in the oven (this method is easiest and quite tasty).

If you've gone to all the trouble of making your own corn nuts, you might just want to toss them with grated Mexican *queso añejo* (or Parmesan) and chopped cilantro.

2 cups (10 ounces) dried corn (see Cook's
Notes)
Vegetable oil to a depth of ¾ inch in a 9- to
10-inch *deep* skillet for oil-toasting
OR a little vegetable oil for oven-toasting
Coarse (kosher) salt

Pour the corn into a medium bowl, cover generously with tap water, cover and refrigerate for 3 days.

Drain the corn thoroughly and pat it dry on paper towels; it needs to be dry to the touch.

For oil-toasting: In the deep skillet, heat ¾ inch of oil to 360 degrees (it's best to use a thermometer to ensure that it's hot enough—the oil will shimmer slightly on the surface when it reaches this temperature, and a tiny droplet of water added to the hot oil will splatter and pop). A spoonful at a time, add the dried corn to the oil. The oil will immediately bubble up and the corn will float to the top. Stir it around every once in a while as it toasts to a golden crunchiness, about 9 minutes. You'll know that the corn is ready when it's deeply golden and most of the bubbles have subsided. Drain on paper towels and, while hot, toss with salt.

For oven-toasting: Heat the oven to 400 degrees. Toss the dried corn with enough oil to give it a rich, shiny coating and spread the corn on a baking sheet lined with parchment or a nonstick baking mat. Bake until the corn nuts are richly golden and crunchy, 50 minutes to an hour. Toss with salt.

If you're not serving the corn nuts right away, cool them completely and store in an airtight container for up to a week at room temperature or for several months in the freezer.

Index

Note: Page numbers in *italic* type refer to photographs.

allspice:

    salt, in tangerine spice margarita, *28*, 29–30

    salt, preparing, 28

    in smoky spiced cashews, *214*, 216

    in spiced salt, 127

allspice dram, in tangerine spice margarita, *28*, 29–30

almond butter, in almond-grapefruit guacamole, 187–89, *188*

almond(s):

    in coconut *horchata*, 136–37

    -grapefruit guacamole, 187–89, *188*

ancho chiles:

    powdered, 203

    in tequila old-fashioned, 106, 107–8

añejo tequila:

    about, 5

    aging times, 79

    in coconut-vanilla *horchata* cocktail, 152–54, *153*

    flavors of, 79

    in my idea of the best splurge margarita, 17–20, *18*

    in port sangría, 120–21

    tasting notes, 96

    in tequila old-fashioned, *106*, 107–8

    in today's perfect margarita (aka Topolo margarita), *10*, 11

Aperol:

    in the bitter truth, 117–19, *118*

    in the ultimate strawberry margarita, *44*, 45–46

    in watermelon cocktail, 131, *132*

apple brandy:

    in apple-habanero margarita, 61–63, *62*

    in apple-tamarind cocktail, 127–28

    in caramel apple cocktail, 146–47

apple cider:

    in apple-tamarind cocktail, 127–28

    in caramel apple cocktail, 146–47

apple(s):

    -fennel guacamole, 186

    flavoring cocktails with, 27

    flavoring guacamole with, 165

    -habanero margarita, 61–63, *62*

    -habanero puree, 64

    -tamarind cocktail, 127–28

árbol chiles:

    in brown butter guacamole with porcini and crab, 196–98, *197*

    in limey red chile napa cabbage, 212

avocados:

    about, 159

    in almond-grapefruit guacamole, 187–89, *188*

    in apple-fennel guacamole, 186

    in brown butter guacamole with porcini and crab, 196–98, *197*

    in classic guacamole, 160–61

    in grilled corn and poblano guacamole, 174–76, *175*

    in guacamole with bacon, grilled ramps (or green onions) and roasted tomatillos, 167–68, *169*

    in guacamole with strawberries and habanero, 172, *173*

extra-añejo tequila:
    about, 5
    aging times, 79

F

fall recipes:
    jamaica–prickly pear (cactus fruit)
        margarita, 65–68, *67, 69*
    apple-habanero margarita, 61–63, *62*
fennel:
    -apple guacamole, 186
    flavoring guacamole with, 165
framboise liqueur, in raspberry-lemongrass
    margarita, 53–55, *54*
Friday special:
    orange–passion fruit cocktail, 133–34, *135*
Frontera's sweet-and-sour mix (aka
    limonada), 21
fruits. *See also specific fruits*
    citrusy jícama and watermelon with
        toasted sesame, 207–9, *208*
    lime-pickled melon, 205, *206*
    for seasonal margaritas, 25–27

G

ginger:
    agave syrup, 40
    beer syrup, homemade, 112
    beer syrup, in Mexican el diablo, 109–11,
        110
    flavoring cocktails with, 25
    margarita, sparkling, *38*, 39–40
    in tangy cucumber-mint cocktail, 129–30
    -watermelon guacamole, *180*, 181–82

ginger liqueur, in tangy cucumber-mint
    cocktail, 129–30
gold leaf flakes, in my idea of the best splurge
    margarita, 17–20, *18*
Grand Marnier:
    flavor of, 6
    in my idea of the best splurge margarita,
        17–20, *18*
    tasting notes, 97
Gran Gala brandy, 6
grapefruit:
    -almond guacamole, 187–89, *188*
    in el mural, *90*, 91–92
    flavoring guacamole with, 165–66
green chile:
    "pickled" chayote, 210, *211*
    pumpkin seeds with tequila and lime, 213,
        214
    –sesame pecans, *214*, 215
green onions, grilled (or ramps), bacon and
    roasted tomatillos, guacamole with,
    167–68, *169*
grilled corn and poblano guacamole, 174–76,
    175
grilled pineapple–vanilla puree, 76
grilled ramps (or green onions), bacon and
    roasted tomatillos, guacamole with,
    167–68, *169*
guacamole:
    about, 164–66
    almond-grapefruit, 187–89, *188*
    apple-fennel, 186
    with bacon, grilled ramps (or green onions)
        and roasted tomatillos, 167–68, *169*

roasted, guacamole with blackberry-
mezcal jewels, 177–79, *178*
in roasted tomatillo salsa, 163
seeding and chopping, *161*
in watermelon-ginger guacamole, *180*,
181–82
jamaica:
—prickly pear (cactus fruit) margarita,
65–68, *67, 69*
sugar, preparing, 65
tequila, 66
jícama:
cucumber, and crushed chile, pineapple
margarita with, 41–42, *43*
and watermelon, citrusy, with toasted
sesame, 207–9, *208*
juniper tequila:
in juniper tequila and tonic, 103
in Mr. B, 105
recipe for, 104

K

kaffir lime leaf, in sparkling ginger
margarita, *38*, 39–40
Kahlúa, in café Tacuba, 143–45, *144*
Key limes:
in classic recipe for the margarita, 6–7
flavor of, 3–4

L

lemongrass:
in homemade ginger beer syrup, 112
in homemade tonic syrup, 104
-raspberry margarita, 53–55, *54*
-raspberry tequila, 56

lemon(s), Meyer
flavoring cocktails with, 25
margarita, 32, 33–35
simple syrup, 37
tequila, 36, 37
tequila, in Meyer lemon margarita, 32,
33–35
lemon twist, making, 33, *35*
lime(s). *See also limonada*
in absinthe-mezcal margarita, 93–94
in apple-habanero margarita, 61–63, *62*
in apple-tamarind cocktail, 127–28
in the best margarita on a budget, 12–13
(or orange) bitters, 88–89, *89*
in black currant–rhubarb margarita, 47–48
choosing, for margaritas, 3–5
in cilantro-jalapeño margarita, 57–59, *58*
in citrusy jícama and watermelon with
toasted sesame, 207–9, *208*
in coconut-vanilla *horchata* cocktail, 152–
54, *153*
crushing skin on, 4
in el mural, *90*, 91–92
in homemade ginger beer syrup, 112
in homemade sangrita, 116
in homemade sweet-and-sour mix, 5
in homemade tonic syrup, 104
in *jamaica*–prickly pear (cactus fruit)
margarita, 65–68, *67, 69*
in juniper tequila and tonic, 103
Key, flavor of, 3–4
Key, in classic recipe for the margarita, 6–7
in limey red chile napa cabbage, 212
in Mexican el diablo, 109–11, *110*
in Oaxacan gold margarita, 75

lime(s) (*continued*)
   in orange–passion fruit cocktail, 133–34, *135*
   in peach (or mango)-basil margarita, 49–51, *50*
   -pickled melon, 205, *206*
   in pineapple margarita with jícama, cucumber and crushed chile, 41–42, *43*
   range of flavors, 4
   ripening process, 4
   in sparkling ginger margarita, *38*, 39–40
   squeezing ahead of time, 4–5
   squeezing juice from, 4
   in tangerine spice margarita, *28*, 29–30
   in tangy cucumber-mint *agua fresca*, 129
   in today's perfect margarita (aka Topolo margarita), *10*, 11
   in the ultimate strawberry margarita, *44*, 45–46
   -watermelon *agua fresca*, 131
limonada:
   aka Frontera's sweet-and-sour mix, 21
   in the bitter truth, 117–19, *118*
   in mezcal margarita #2, 85–87, *86*
   in my idea of the best splurge margarita, 17–20, *18*
   in port sangría, 120–21
   in raspberry-lemongrass margarita, 53–55, *54*
   in today's perfect margarita (aka Topolo margarita), *10*, 11

M

mango (or peach)-basil margarita, 49–51, *50*

margaritas. *See also* classic margaritas; mezcal margaritas; seasonal fruit and herb margaritas
   ingredients in, 3–6
   master class in, 3–8
   proportions for, 6–7
   salting rims for, 7–8
   shaking, importance of, 7
measuring, 9
melon. *See also* watermelon
   lime-pickled, 205, *206*
Mexican el diablo, 109–11, *110*
Meyer lemon(s):
   flavoring cocktails with, 25
   margarita, *32*, 33–35
   simple syrup, 37
   tequila, *36*, 37
   tequila, in Meyer lemon margarita, *32*, 33–35
mezcal. *See also* mezcal margaritas
   about, 79–80
   -blackberry jewels, 179
   classifications of, 79–80
   compared with tequila, 77–78
   Denomination of Origin names, 78
   flavor of, 73, 80
   from Oaxaca, about, 78, 80
   tasting notes, 96–97
mezcal margaritas:
   about, 73–74
   absinthe-mezcal margarita, 93–94
   el mural, *90*, 91–92
   mezcal margarita #2, 85–87, *86*
   Oaxacan gold margarita, 75
   tamarind-mezcal margarita, 81–83, *82*

milk, in twenty-four-hour *cajeta*, 147
mint:
    in absinthe-mezcal margarita, 93–94
    -cucumber *agua fresca*, tangy, 129
    -cucumber cocktail, tangy, 129–30
    in roasted jalapeño guacamole with
      blackberry-mezcal jewels, 177–79, *178*
modern tequila cocktails:
    about, 101–2
    the bitter truth, 117–19, *118*
    juniper tequila and tonic, 103
    Mexican el diablo, 109–11, *110*
    Mr. B, 105
    port sangría, 120–21
    tequila old-fashioned, *106*, 107–8
    vampiro, 113–15, *114*
Mr. B, 105
mushrooms, in brown butter guacamole with
    porcini and crab, 196–98, *197*
my idea of the best splurge margarita, 17–20, *18*

N
nut and seed snacks:
    about, 203–4
    green chile pumpkin seeds with tequila
      and lime, 213, *214*
    homemade corn nuts, 217–18
    sesame–green chile pecans, *214*, 215
    smoky spiced cashews, *214*, 216
nuts:
    in almond-grapefruit guacamole, 187–89,
      188
    in coconut *horchata*, 136–37
    in guacamole with toasted walnuts and
      pomegranate, 193–95, *194*

sesame–green chile pecans, *214*, 215
smoky spiced cashews, *214*, 216

O
Oaxacan gold margarita, 75
old-fashioned, tequila, *106*, 107–8
onions, green, grilled (or ramps), bacon and
    roasted tomatillos, guacamole with,
    167–68, *169*
orange bitters, 88–89
    in mezcal margarita #2, 85–87, *86*
    in tequila old-fashioned, *106*, 107–8
orange Curaçao:
    in absinthe-mezcal margarita, 93–94
    in *jamaica*–prickly pear (cactus fruit)
      margarita, 65–68, *67*, *69*
    in sparkling ginger margarita, *38*, 39–40
    tasting notes, 97
orange-infused brandy:
    in black currant–rhubarb margarita,
      47–48
    in my idea of the best splurge margarita,
      17–20, *18*
    tasting notes, 97
    in today's perfect margarita (aka Topolo
      margarita), *10*, 11
orange liqueurs. *See also* orange-infused
    brandy; triple sec
    choosing, for margaritas, 6
    in classic recipe for the margarita, 6–7
    tasting notes, 97
orange(s):
    (or lime) bitters, 88–89
    in citrusy jícama and watermelon with
      toasted sesame, 207–9, *208*

spiced, in tangerine spice margarita, *28*,
    29–30
tamarind-mezcal margarita, 81–83, *82*
tasting notes, 97
vanilla, in the best margarita on a budget,
    12–13
vanilla, preparing, 11
Tuesday special:
    apple-tamarind cocktail, 127–28
twenty-four-hour *cajeta*, 147

U

the ultimate strawberry margarita, *44*,
    45–46

V

vampiro, 113–15, *114*
vanilla:
    -coconut *horchata* cocktail, 152–54, *153*
    –grilled pineapple puree, 76
    –grilled pineapple puree, in Oaxacan gold
        margarita, 75
    triple sec, in the best margarita on a
        budget, 12–13
    triple sec, preparing, 11
vegetable and fruit snacks:
    about, 203–4
    citrusy jícama and watermelon with
        toasted sesame, 207–9, *208*
    green chile "pickled" chayote, 210, *211*
    lime-pickled melon, 205, *206*

limey red chile napa cabbage, 212
vegetable(s). *See also specific vegetables*
    citrusy jícama and watermelon with
        toasted sesame, 207–9, *208*
    green chile "pickled" chayote, 210, *211*
    pickled, and heirloom tomato guacamole,
        183–85, *184*
vermouth, in Mr. B, 105

W

walnuts, toasted, and pomegranate,
    guacamole with, 193–95, *194*
watercress and sesame, guacamole with,
    170–71
watermelon:
    cocktail, 131, *132*
    flavoring guacamole with, 165
    -ginger guacamole, *180*, 181–82
    and jícama, citrusy, with toasted sesame,
        207–9, *208*
    -lime *agua fresca*, 131
Wednesday special:
    tangy cucumber-mint cocktail, 129–30
wine, in sparkling ginger margarita, *38*,
    39–40
winter recipes:
    Meyer lemon margarita, *32*, 33–35
    pineapple margarita with jícama,
        cucumber and crushed chile, 41–42, *43*
    sparkling ginger margarita, *38*, 39–40
    tangerine spice margarita, *28*, 29–30

About the Authors

RICK BAYLESS is the author of eight cookbooks, including *Mexican Everyday* and *Fiesta at Rick's*. Rick won Bravo's Top Chef Masters competition and was named National Chef of the Year by the James Beard Foundation. The Mexican government has awarded Rick the Order of the Aztec Eagle, the highest decoration given to foreigners. He owns and operates three award-winning restaurants in Chicago: the casual Frontera Grill, named Outstanding Restaurant of the Year by the James Beard Foundation; the four-star dining Topolobampo; and XOCO, a LEED Gold-certified quick-serve restaurant. He lives in Chicago with his wife, Deann Groen Bayless.

DEANN GROEN BAYLESS has coauthored eight books with Rick and co-owns and co-operates Frontera Grill, Topolobampo, and XOCO with him. She is a former president of Women Chefs and Restaurateurs, a national organization that promotes the education and advancement of women in the restaurant industry, and is the administrator of the Frontera Farmer Foundation.